1.00 .

CHINA'S PLAN TO DOMINATE
ASIA AND THE WORLD
HEGEMON

STEVEN W. MOSHER

ENCOUNTER BOOKS
SAN FRANCISCO

Published by Encounter Books, an activity of Encounter for Culture and Education, Inc., a nonprofit tax exempt corporation.

Encounter Books website address: www.encounterbooks.com

Cover and text design © Ayelet Maida, A/M Studios.
Calligraphy by You Shan Tang. The Chinese character *pà:* To rule by might rather than by right.
Dragon image from PhotoDisc.

Manufactured in the United States of America.
The paper used in this publication meets the minimum requirements of ANSI/NISO Z39.48-1992 (R 1997) (Permanence of Paper).

Library of Congress Cataloging-in-Publication Data
Mosher, Steven W. 1948–
    Hegemon: China's plan to dominate Asia and the world / Steven W. Mosher.
        p. cm.
    Includes bibliographical references and index.
    ISBN 1-893554-08-2 (cloth : alk. paper)
1. China—Relations—Foreign countries.   I. Title.
    DS740.4.M67 2000
    327.51'009—cd21
                                                            00-028283

10   9   8   7   6   5   4   3   2   1

Contents

The Tiananmen Temptation

M ay you live in interesting times. This phrase may resonate pleasantly in the Western ear, but it is a curse in China. For "interesting times," in the vast sweep of Chinese history, has all too often been a polite euphemism for the chaos of armed banditry and rebellion that envelops a corrupt and dying dynasty. It connotes a state of social confusion and mortal danger that one would only wish on one's enemies.

My own life and times have been far from dull where the People's Republic of China is concerned. Following Deng Xiaoping's wrenching opening to the West, I became the first American social scientist allowed to conduct a full-length study of a Chinese village, only to be declared an "international spy" and asked to leave the country.

In March of 1979 I first arrived, elated yet diffident, in the village of Xingchai, which would be my home for much of the next two years. My stay there was a series of "interesting" surprises. Thirty years of incessant political campaigns, I discovered, had deeply scarred the Chinese people. Mao Zedong's Cultural Revolution, although still defended by pockets of intellectual resistance in the West, had been a disaster of the first magnitude, killing millions and leaving many millions more of walking wounded in its wake. The one-child policy, which erupted onto the Chinese landscape while I was there, came right out of Mao's playbook, an uncomfortable reminder of how far the regime was still willing to go in its pursuit of utopian goals. I left China in 1980 with pleas for help from Chinese women I had worked with still ringing in my ears, very much aware of how China's totalitarian past still overshadowed its present and determined its future. The fact that I had been arrested some days before my departure on specious charges of "violating the travel regulations for foreigners" and put under house arrest until I wrote a "confession" was further confirmation of this dark heritage.

Still, like many observers of China, by the late eighties I had fallen into what I have come to think of since as the Tiananmen Temptation. This was the comforting notion that the forces unleashed by Deng Xiaoping's economic reform were leading China not merely in the direction of capitalism, but also toward freedom.

I was heartened by images of one million demonstrators on the streets of Beijing, particularly when I remembered the cowed and fearful peasants I had known a decade earlier. The Chinese people, in their powerful mass, had at last stood up. The Tiananmen demonstrations seemed to be good news not only for those of us who felt an emotional connection to this country, but also for U.S. national interests. The dream-like appearance of the Goddess of Democracy in Tiananmen Square seemed to confirm that China would change before it became powerful, that the People's Republic would democratize before the U.S. was forced to confront its ambitions. I was not alone in interpreting the bloodbath that followed as the horrifying last gasp of an *ancien régime,* which would soon be replaced by a government not only more tolerant of dissent but perhaps even ready to embark upon serious political reform.

The frequent reference to American democratic ideals—popular sovereignty, inalienable rights, limited government and the rule of law—made by Chinese dissidents both inside and outside of China during that time of turmoil seemed to be proof that economic changes had allowed Western ideals to take root in Chinese soil more quickly than even the most optimistic American triumphalists would have thought possible. The ranks of the democrats were constantly being augmented, I believed, as the economic reforms of the eighties was strengthened and deepened in the early nineties. The advent of the Internet, making communication with ordinary Chinese possible, would further speed the process of political change. I rested my hope for a fruitful and peaceable relationship between the U.S. and the Middle Kingdom on the rise of pro-freedom, pro–free enterprise forces within it. China's continued economic expansion and foreign trade would stimulate the growth of middle and entrepreneurial classes interested in peacefully improving their lot in life. The martyrs of Tiananmen Square would become China's Founding Fathers. My assumption was that the Communist Party was moribund and that a democratic revolution was inevitable.

The last few years have revealed how chimerical these hopes were. Those forces which appeared to be driving China toward openness have all been spent or checked. The Chinese Communist Party now has a firmer grip on power than ever. Inside China, dissident groups were crushed so completely that within a couple of years they effectively ceased to exist. Outside of China, the thousands of exile groups that sprang up in solidarity with what they envisioned as a great internal awakening became demoralized and began to evaporate. While this occurred partly through normal attrition, some groups were torn apart by dissension, fostered in part by Chinese Communist agents who penetrated the organizations and worked to sow division within their ranks. Others were hollowed out as their leaders, one by one, made a separate peace with Beijing in order to engage in the China trade or visit their families. The condition for being allowed to return to China may sound bland, but it was chilling to anyone who heard the message behind the words: "You must not make statements unfriendly to China."

What of the optimistic theory that the ongoing economic reform would create competing centers of economic, social, and eventually political power, weakening the hold of the Chinese Communist party? There is a new middle class, but it evinces little interest in politics, concentrating instead on the prospect, as Deng Xiaoping so bluntly put it, of "getting rich." To display this carrot, after using the bloody stick, Deng deliberately brought the Chinese economy to a boil after the Tiananmen demonstrations. It was distraction, albeit on a massive scale, and it worked. Millions of Chinese set aside their dreams of freedom and went scrambling after Deng's dream of riches. With the Chinese economy booming along year after year, there seemed little point in protesting against the government. This was China's version of "It's the economy, stupid."

The momentum generated by these economic reforms was quickly hijacked by the Communist Party elite. The most successful entrepreneurs in China today are the "princelings," who have prospered because of their connections to China's leading families and to the bureaucratic powers. Instead of constituting a separate center of liberalized economic, social and, eventually, political influence, as the hopeful scenarios following Tiananmen had it, the beneficiaries of the new wealth reinforce the existing regime. How likely is Deng Xiaoping's grandson to rebel against the system that his grandfather helped to create, and that his family benefits from? China is today governed by an elite that controls the state sector directly and the private sector, or at least its most profitable areas, indirectly.

And what of the students, who so bravely led the demonstrations a decade ago? We think of change in China happening in linear fashion, with each new generation more Western-oriented and democratically-minded than the last. But the generation of Chinese now coming of age is in fact more patriotic, more resentful of the U.S. and more favorably disposed towards the current Chinese leadership than the generation of Tiananmen.

The Tiananmen generation was born in the sixties and early seventies, during the Cultural Revolution. Its earliest memories were of the turmoil and violence of that experience, and open warfare among competing Red Guard factions, with son set against father and brother against brother. The coming of age of this generation took place against a backdrop of bitter criticism of the homicidal policies of Chairman Mao. Its leaders were in school when the Chinese Communist Party repudiated much of its own past. They were disaffected from their own leaders, deaf to Maoist cant, and open in a unique way to ideas from abroad on how to organize society to foster human freedom. When Tiananmen began, they took to the streets in large numbers to give voice to their disaffection and to call for an end to corruption, bureaucracy, and dictatorship.

The next generation—the present one—are the children of the economic reform and the political backlash that followed Tiananmen. Born in the late seventies and early eighties, when the chaos of Maoism was just a receding memory, they have known only stability and increasing prosperity. In their minds, Tiananmen has been distorted into an outbreak of chaos like the Cultural Revolution, though it was nothing of the sort. When they ponder it at all, it seems to them both a warning and a curse. Their political education has veered away from ideology in favor of nationalism: they have been made familiar with the glories of China's imperial past, and with the history of her humiliation at the hands of the Western powers. They have been taught, and have come to believe, that America is denying China her rightful place in the world.

Yet illusions about China die hard. When U.S. Ambassador James Sasser went to speak at Tianjin University on the occasion of President Clinton's 1998 visit to China, he expected a respectful hearing from the students, believing them to be China's "agents of change." Instead, he got an unscripted grilling from a surprisingly nationalistic audience which aggressively, and with considerable hostility, questioned him about America's presence in Asia and support for Taiwan.

On such questions, there is no division between these young students and the masters of China's universe. Had the students been asked, they would have vigorously endorsed China's Defense White Paper, issued in July 1998, in which Beijing's strategic planners insist that China must "lead the world into the twenty-first century." Like the drafters of the white paper, the students who confronted Ambassador Sasser identify all of China's most pressing security problems with the U.S. presence in Asia and U.S. dominance of world affairs. These young superpatriots want China to be the supreme power in the world. They believe, above all, there can only be one Hegemon.

CHAPTER ONE

Western Barbarians

To govern a large state is like cooking a small fish.
Stir as little as possible.

—Lao Zi, *Daode Jing*

T he role of the Hegemon is deeply embedded in China's national dreamwork, intrinsic to its national identity, and
profoundly implicated in its sense of national destiny. An unwill-
ingness to concede dominance to any foreign power is deeply rooted
in China's imperial past as the dominant power of Asia and in
the ongoing certainty of the Chinese that they are culturally superior to other peoples.

The concept of hegemony was, fittingly enough, introduced into
modern diplomatic discourse by the Chinese themselves. During
Henry Kissinger's secret visit to Beijing in 1971, the Chinese trans-
lator's use of this unfamiliar English word sent the Americans
scrambling for their dictionaries. They found definitions of "hegemony" as "a single pole or axis of power," or as "leadership or
predominant influence exercised by one state over others."

None of these definitions fully captures the rich and sometimes sinister nuances of this concept, the *Ba*, in Chinese. The
Ba is a political order invented by ancient Chinese strategists 2,800
years ago which is based exclusively on naked power. Under the
Ba, as it evolved over the next six centuries, total control of a state's
population and resources was to be concentrated in the hands of
the state's hegemon, or *Bawang* (literally "hegemon-king"), who
would in turn employ it to establish his hegemony, or *Baquan*

(literally "hegemon-power"), over all the states in the known world. To put it in modern parlance, Chinese strategists of old may be said to have invented totalitarianism more than two millennia before Lenin introduced it to the West, in order to achieve a kind of super-superpower status.[1]

Totalitarianism has become all too familiar as a concept in recent world history. Still somewhat exotic is hegemony: the non-Western notion that the premier goal of foreign policy should be to establish absolute dominance over one's region and, by slow extension, the world. In a sense, hegemony is the *natural* external expression of totalitarianism, with disputes involving unabsorbed territories resolved by the threat and, if necessary, the reality of force, just as the *natural* expression of democracy is peaceful, neighborly relations, with disputes resolved by negotiation and treaty.

Throughout the 70s and 80s, the Chinese untiringly accused the Soviet Union of having "hegemonic" ambitions. Following the Soviet collapse, they turned their wrath on the U.S., ominously and repeatedly charging that America was "seeking hegemony." In fact, all this name calling was a political form of Freudian projection, for China's elite clearly covets the title of Hegemon for itself.

In the old—and enduring—Chinese view of the world, chaos and disorder can only be avoided by organizing vassal and tributary states around a single, dominant axis of power. And if there is to be a Hegemon, Chinese history and culture combine to say, then it should be China. In their obsession with the Hegemon, the Chinese people have their own doctrine of manifest destiny.

For more than two thousand years the Chinese considered themselves the geographical, and geopolitical, center of the world.[2] From their earliest incarnation as an empire they spoke of China as *Zhong Guo*, "The Middle Kingdom," or even more revealingly, as *Tian Xia*, "Everything Under Heaven." They believed their emperor to be the only legitimate political authority in their known world and viewed themselves as the highest expression of civilized humanity. This Sinocentric worldview survived even foreign invasion and occupation by Jurchens, Mongols, and Manchus, since the Chinese were invariably able to subdue or assimilate their poorly organized and culturally inferior conquerors within a generation or two.

Far from being a self-serving myth or shallow chauvinism, China's idea of national greatness is firmly rooted in reality. For most of its long history, the Chinese empire was indeed a collection of superlatives. It had the greatest land area, the largest population, the most productive economy, the most powerful army, and the most advanced technology of any power on earth. China's sway was limited only by its own ambitions, not by the counterforce of hostile and competing powers. The poorly organized barbarians who populated the border regions were regarded as inferior in every way by the culturally superior Chinese. Under aggressive emperors, the Middle Kingdom quickly grew to the geographical limit—in the days when communications were limited to the speed of a galloping horse—of what could be governed from a single center. With the possible exception of the Roman Empire at its height, the realms of the major Chinese dynasties dwarfed in population and geographic extent all contemporaneous empires in other parts of the world.

By the mid–Qing dynasty (1644–1911), China held sway over a vast territory stretching from today's Russian Far East, westward across southern Siberia to Lake Balkhash and into contemporary Kazakhstan, then southeastward along the Himalayas to the Indian Ocean, and then eastward across Laos and northern Vietnam. Vassal and tributary states, which further extended the reach of the imperial court, included Korea, Tibet, Nepal, Burma, Thailand, and parts of Indochina.

Toward these subordinate states, Imperial China behaved as a suzerain, exacting tribute, imposing unequal conditions, and demanding fealty from their rulers. Those who refused to kowtow to Beijing were regarded as hostile and dealt with accordingly. The Celestial Empire had neighbors only in a geographic sense. Even today, as Ross Munro has observed, China still seems to classify her "neighbors" into one of two categories: tributary states that acknowledge her hegemony, or potential enemies.[3] Present-day Beijing does not desire equality in external affairs, but deference, for it governs not a nation-state—although that is the pretense—but an all-encompassing civilization.

RELATIONS WITH THE BARBARIANS

The first Westerners to reach China by sea were the Portuguese, who by 1557 had established a permanent settlement at Macao. The Spaniards, the Dutch, and the British followed, drawn by the prospect of trade with this huge and prosperous empire. But the Imperial Chinese government, first under the Ming dynasty (1368–1644), then under the Qing, permitted only limited commercial relations with these seafaring traders. Canton, the capital of Guangdong province, was designated as China's sole entrepôt for the western trade, and even here trading was limited to a clearly defined season.

These inconvenient, even degrading, arrangements were repeatedly protested by the Western nations, whose emissaries vainly called for free trade and diplomatic representation in Beijing. But they received short shrift. The volume of its trade with the West was insignificant to the vast Chinese empire, while direct government-to-government relations were out of the question. The early Qing emperors and their courts were affronted by the notion that they should deal with the "Barbarians from the Western Oceans" on a basis of equality. Instead, as an emblem of their disdain, they gave a mere provincial official, the Viceroy of Guangdong and Guangxi, responsibility for political and commercial relations with these pushy Westerners.

As long as the Qing Empire stayed strong, there matters remained. But by the end of the eighteenth century, the dynasty was clearly in decline, and over the succeeding decades the government became increasingly inefficient, weak, and corrupt. The power of the Western world, on the other hand, was on the ascendant, fueled by industrialization and scientific advances. The First and Second Opium Wars (1839–42 and 1856–60), and the unequal treaties that resulted, reduced China to a semicolony of the Western powers. Western troops garrisoned the treaty ports and Western gunboats roamed her rivers. Only the Open Door policy of the U.S., which opposed the creation of exclusive economic zones by the other great powers, saved China from total dismemberment.

Non-Chinese have difficulty appreciating the depth of China's grievances against the West resulting from this experience. It was not merely that Western gunboats twice defeated China in the Opium Wars; China had been defeated before, although never perhaps by organized drug runners. Nor was the bitterness caused simply by the dethronement of Confucian high culture by the West, although this assault comes closer to the heart of China's wounded pride. China had dominated (in every sense—culturally, economically, militarily) its "known world" almost since the beginning of its recorded history. More than what is today called a superpower, it had been *the* hegemon, for dynasty after dynasty, for over two thousand years. Then, from this pinnacle of greatness, it was brought low by the Western powers, divided into spheres of influence, and very nearly carved up into colonies.[4]

When Mao Zedong announced the establishment of the People's Republic of China, it was with the words "China has stood up." No longer would China be bullied by the West. So strong was Mao's sense of grievance that, despite his continuing desperate need for Soviet economic assistance, he rejected Khrushchev's bid for Soviet naval bases in China. When the Soviet leader petulantly objected that America's allies allowed the U.S. Navy basing privileges, Mao still refused to budge. Foreign naval vessels would never be stationed in Chinese waters again, he declared. That degrading experience belonged to China's treaty port past.

Both the history of China's imperial—and revolutionary—glory and the painful details of her long night of national humiliation are taught in China's public schools and, more importantly, in her military academies. The result is an excruciating sensitivity to slights, real and imagined. When Secretary of State Warren Christopher visited China in 1994, Chinese officials were aghast that he had brought his dog. Why? Because a *century* ago, purportedly, a sign had hung at the entrance to a park in Shanghai's foreign concession reading "No dogs or Chinese allowed."

China's fall from greatness is still a subliminal matter of shame for all living Chinese. This "loss of face" cannot be assuaged merely by allowing China to take its place among "the family of nations." The rectification of China's historical grievances requires not merely diplomatic equality—Beijing enjoys this already—but de facto geostrategic dominance. The lowering of the Union Jack in Hong Kong was a start, redeeming China's painful humiliation at the hands of the British in the Opium Wars. But only one thing will completely lift the burden of shame: for the Celestial Empire to resume its rightful place as the natural center of the world.

USING AMERICAN POWER TO DEFEAT AMERICAN HEGEMONY

It was not only on the issue of naval bases that the Chinese Communist Party elite resisted its overbearing Soviet "older brothers." Despite the ideological kinship with the Soviet Union, they feared that they would be permanently dominated within this sibling relationship. The alliance was to all outward appearances as close as "lips and teeth," in the Chinese phrase, but China was increasingly resentful of Russian claims of superiority for the Soviet model. With the Sino-Soviet split, the old images of Russia as "the hungry land"—*Eguo* in Chinese—were revived, and the traditional contempt of the Chinese for the barbarians of the north was once again openly expressed.

China's challenge to Soviet hegemony led it to seek an alliance of convenience with the United States, an ideological foe which it viewed—and continues to view—as a power in decline. This pseudoalliance, never formalized, lasted from the early seventies to the late eighties, when it suddenly received three death blows. The first and most serious was the sudden implosion of the Soviet Union, which robbed the pseudoallies of a common foe and knocked the principal strategic prop out from under the U.S.-China relationship. The second was the Tiananmen Square demonstrations for democracy which, ending in a bloody debacle, highlighted for China's leaders the dangers of uncritically exposing Chinese youth to the appeal of American democratic ideals. The third was America's virtually bloodless victory in the Gulf War, which underlined the unmatched global reach of the U.S. military as well as its technological superiority over other countries.

Just as China would not accept—indeed, was moved by its own sense of greatness to challenge—Soviet hegemony, so it has refused to accept the U.S. as the world's leading power, but has been moved by that same innate pride to challenge it. Since the early 90's, China has become ever less coy about its intentions. The state-controlled press has grown increasingly strident in denouncing the U.S., calling it everything from "a dangerous enemy" and "a superpower bully," to a "hegemon on par with Nazi Germany."[5] More to the point, America is now the enemy of choice in war games conducted by the People's Liberation Army. In the spring of 2000, after threatening to use force against Taiwan to "unify" it with the mainland, the official newspaper of the PLA also warned that it was ready to use its long range missiles against the United States if it came to the island's aid.

The one way in which China, until lately, continued to value America's role in Asia was as a regional stabilizer. America's postwar military presence in Japan was not unwelcome, for in the Chinese view it served to keep Japan militarily weak. For decades, Beijing feared that a U.S. withdrawal would precipitate Japan's rearmament and eventual reemergence as a major military power. Since the mid-nineties, however, with the Japanese economy in a deep recession and its own power on the mainland of Asia growing rapidly, China has grown increasingly confident of its ability to dominate the region and has ratcheted up its criticism of the U.S. presence accordingly.

The Chinese so relentlessly accuse the U.S. of "seeking hegemony," and phrase their accusations in such condemnatory terms, that many analysts have concluded that the word "hegemony" is strictly pejorative in Chinese usage. Nothing could be further from the truth. In the view of Chinese strategists, the existence of a hegemon is in fact a natural, even a desirable state of affairs. Following the Spring and Autumn period (772–481 B.C.), when the institution of hegemon first developed, it gradually produced stability, order, and equilibrium in the Middle Kingdom, as neighboring states were absorbed into a single entity. It is the division of the strategic landscape into states large and small that is undesirable, for it leads to instability and chaos. The lesson China draws from its long history is that periods of division are times of disorder and chaos, whereas periods of unity are times of stability and order. In other words, China needs a Hegemon.

That China has an extraordinary fear of chaos and penchant for unity is widely understood. What is less well appreciated is that China projects its own 5,000-year history onto the wider contemporary world and reaches that same conclusion: The world needs a Hegemon. To put it another way, for Chinese strategists, balance-of-power politics is inherently unbalanced. Racial pride, an innate sense of cultural superiority, and a long history all tell the Chinese that the role of Hegemon properly belongs to China and its rulers.

Thus the current debate over American China policy, whether we should "engage" China or attempt to "contain" it, misses the essential point. From the Chinese perspective, the U.S. is already "containing" China by its very presence in Asia, by maintaining 100,000 troops in the region, by its network of bases and its alliances with Japan and the Republic of Korea. That the U.S. did not seek its preeminent position, but in many respects had its international role thrust upon it following World War II and reinforced by its sudden victory in the Cold War, makes the situation that much more intolerable for those anxious to restore China's lost glory. That Providence smiles upon America may be an old story for Americans, but it is one that is difficult for Chinese to appreciate. So is the American ideal of leadership. For example, the insouciance of General Washington to those who would make him king renders his character opaque to most Chinese. Surely, they conclude, he was plotting for the office all along, according to the wisdom of the ancient strategist Sun-tzu: When seeking power, make it appear that you are not doing so.

Read between the lines of Chinese criticism of America's leading role in the world and one finds the envy and enmity that come from balked ambition. The *People's Daily*, the official organ of the Chinese Communist Party, says that "The U.S. strategic aim is to seek hegemony in the whole world and it cannot tolerate the appearance of any big power on the European and Asian continents that will constitute a threat to its leading position."[6] Can anyone doubt that the "big power" that has "appeared" on the

"Asian continent" referred to here is China itself, moving to over-take America's "leading position"?

The belief in the inevitability of Chinese hegemony, held at a deeper level than mere strategy, motivates China to oppose and undermine the current *Pax Americana.* Zbigniew Brzezinski, who as National Security Advisor to President Carter played a key role in the 1979 establishment of U.S.-PRC diplomatic relations, believes that "The task of Chinese policy—in keeping with Sun-tzu's ancient strategic wisdom—is to use American power to peacefully defeat American hegemony."[7]

Sun-tzu also said that all strategy is based on deception, and the Chinese are customarily oblique in defining their ultimate aims. One exception is the recent white paper, *China's National Defense,* which the Chinese government produced in response to American urgings toward greater strategic "transparency." Those who expressed pleasure over its promulgation, happy that the Chinese government was finally complying with our request to be more can-did about its ambitions, should carefully read the document. China's opposition to U.S. dominance, and the global scope of its own ambi-tions, come through loud and clear.

In the opening paragraph of the white paper, China stakes its claim to the next millennium: "Mankind is about to enter the 21st century of its history. It is the aspiration of the Chinese govern-ment and people to lead a peaceful, stable and prosperous world into the new century."[8]

In a subsequent section of the white paper, entitled "The International Security Situation," the Chinese government goes on to list "factors of instability both globally and regionally" that it regards as threats to its future:

1. "Hegemonism and power politics remain the main source of threats to world peace and stability";
2. "cold war mentality and its influence still have a cer-tain currency, and the enlargement of military blocs and the strengthening of military alliances have added factors of instability to international security";

3. "some countries, relying on their military advantages, pose military threat to other countries, even resorting to armed intervention";
4. "the old unfair and irrational international economic order still damages the interests of developing countries";
5. "local conflicts caused by ethnic, religious, territorial, natural resources and other factors arise now and then, and questions left over by history among countries remain unsolved";
6. "terrorism, arms proliferation, smuggling and trafficking in narcotics, environmental pollution, waves of refugees, and other transnational issues also pose new threats to international security."[9]

Though couched cryptically, the first "factor of instability" is a stinging criticism of *Pax Americana.* Translated into plain English, it means that the present U.S. political, economic and military preponderance ("hegemony"), combined with Washington's willingness to exercise it ("power politics"), is a threat to China's national security ("world peace and stability").[10]

The second factor is a veiled reference to the enlargement of NATO and the strengthening of U.S.-Japan defense ties, both of which have alarmed China. In April 1997 China joined Russia in denouncing as (what else?) "Hegemonism" the expansion of NATO to include Poland, Hungary and the Czech Republic, which it also called "impermissible." China objected even more vociferously to the redefinition, in early 1996, of the scope of U.S.-Japanese military cooperation from the narrower "Far East" to a wider "Asia-Pacific." The juxtaposition of these two concerns suggests that China sees the strengthened U.S.-Japan Security Treaty not only as an immediate threat but also, as Brzezinski has suggested, as "a point of departure for an American-dominated Asian system of security aimed at containing China (in which Japan would be a vital linchpin much as Germany was in NATO during the Cold War)."[11] The agreement was widely perceived in Beijing as implicitly bringing Taiwan under the protective umbrella of the U.S.-Japan Security Treaty; so the white paper goes on to assail the incorporation, "directly or indirectly," of "the Taiwan Straits into the security and cooperation sphere of any country or any military alliance as an infringement upon and interference in China's sovereignty."[12]

The "military threats" and "armed intervention" referred to in the third factor mean the 1996 missile crisis in the Taiwan Strait, when Washington warned Beijing of "grave consequences" if it continued to bracket the island with missiles and dispatched two carrier groups to guard Taiwan.

The fourth factor reflects continued Chinese unhappiness with the U.S.-dominated economic order and its institutions, such as the International Monetary Fund, the World Bank, and the World Trade Organization, the last of which China has still not been able to join because of its restrictive trading practices. Stigmatizing the existing economic order as "old, unfair and irrational" at a time when many Asian economies were in free fall, resentful of the tight-money policies of the IMF and fearful of defaulting on World Bank loans helped to raise China's stature in the region. Such criticisms may be part of an on-again, off-again effort to position China as the advocate of the Third World.

The bottom line of this white paper is quite clear. From China's point of view, *all* of its major security concerns arise from the present American dominance on the world stage. Obviously believing that a continuation of the U.S.-dominated international order is not in its national interest, Beijing makes clear that its concerns are not just regional but global, and implies that its goal, in the already quoted words of Deng Xiaoping, "is to build up a new international political and economic order."

Brzezinski's reading of the present situation is worth quoting in full: China's "central objective" is "to dilute American regional power to the point that a diminished America will come to need a regionally dominant China as its ally and eventually even a globally powerful China as its partner."[13] There is abundant evidence, from the white paper quoted above and other sources, that he is absolutely correct in asserting that China's near-term geostrategic goal is "to dilute American regional power." But in suggesting that China's ultimate geostrategic end is a global U.S.-China condominium, however, Brzezinski is merely expressing a pious hope. China's ultimate ambition is not to ally itself with the reigning hegemon, but to succeed it. As he notes elsewhere, "Simply by being what it is and where it is, . . . [America] becomes China's unintentional adversary."[14]

Are our growing difficulties with China merely a matter of the U.S. Seventh Fleet being in the wrong place at the wrong time? Many in the Chinese elite would disagree, having arrived at the conviction that the U.S. is deliberately frustrating their country's resurgence. From their perspective, America is consciously attempting to force the "peaceful evolution" of China into a democratic state. We challenge China's human rights record at every turn, continually threaten economic sanctions, and have set up a surrogate radio broadcasting service, Radio Free Asia, to encourage insurrection. We passed a Taiwan Relations Act, and we sell arms to that "renegade province." We followed with the Hong Kong Relations Act, and our Congressmen fete Martin Lee, the leader of the democratic forces in Hong Kong, when he visits our shores. Such moves inflame China's already deep sense of grievance against the West, and especially against the one country it sees as the cultural heir and imperial successor to the early Great Powers.

As every Chinese schoolchild knows, only a century ago the imperial capital of the Great Qing Dynasty was sacked by "Western barbarians." No wonder that for some Chinese the intransitive verb "to Westernize" carries the same implications that "to vandalize" does in the West, and justifies revenge against these past incursions. Lieutenant General Mi Zhenyu, Vice Commandant of the Academy of Military Sciences, was speaking for the leadership of his country when he recently remarked, "[As for the United States,] for a relatively long time it will be absolutely necessary that we quietly nurse our sense of vengeance. . . . We must conceal our abilities and bide our time."[15]

From Beijing's perspective, the continued U.S. military presence in Asia is an unhappy accident and anachronism, the tail end of a century and a half of Western domination over a region that properly belongs within its own sphere of influence. If most PRC insiders want to reestablish the hegemony that China enjoyed over vast parts of Asia for nearly 2,000 years, some, especially in the military, want to go even further. They are resentful that China has lost its traditional place as the "Central Kingdom" to the world, and are determined to recover it.

For the most part muted, China's impatience to rid Asia of Americans occasionally comes through loud and clear. In February 1995, for instance, when a U.S. carrier task force was ordered to steam up the coast of North Korea into the Bohai Gulf as a warning to Pyongyang to abandon its nuclear weapons program, this show of American naval might so close to its own shores greatly angered Beijing, which ordered a submarine to sortie from the Qingdao naval base and attempt to close on the task force. Detected as soon as it entered the Gulf, the sub was first shadowed and then harassed until it retreated to its home port. Furious Chinese officials issued a threat: If such an incident occurred again, the PLA Navy would be given orders to open fire.

China's resentment is further fueled by wild fantasies about American omnipotence and malice, which are not only given credence by, but actually emanate from, the PRC military and political elite. General Li Jijun, one of China's most distinguished military authors, openly claims that the United States engineered both the collapse of the Soviet Union and the Iraqi invasion of Kuwait by "strategic deceptions." Most of the Chinese leadership apparently believes that the U.S. deliberately bombed the PRC embassy in Belgrade to humiliate China, and that the U.S. is working covertly to "dismember" China, beginning with Tibet and Xinjiang.[16]

All this suggests a PRC which has, in combination, the historical grievances of a Weimar Republic, the paranoid nationalism of a revolutionary Islamic state, and the expansionist ambitions of a Soviet Union at the height of its power. As China grows more powerful, and attempts to rectify those grievances and act out those ambitions, it will cast an ever-lengthening shadow over Asia and the world.

It is often said that America is too democratic at home to be autocratic abroad. Not so China, whose autocratic rulers face few domestic limits on the use of their power abroad. President Jiang Zemin can order his troops into action without a declaration of war by the National People's Congress. He can mobilize the economy to produce weapons of war without the need to convince a skeptical parliament that the expenditures are necessary. And he can command the popular passion by launching internal political campaigns through the Party and the state-owned media.

Few Americans have yet grasped either the depth of China's historic grievances against the West, or its vengeful envy of the U.S. in particular, or the breadth of its resurgent imperial ambitions. But China is not just an emerging superpower with a grudge—though that would be worrisome enough. It is the Hegemon, waiting to reclaim its rightful position as the center of the world.

CHAPTER TWO

Birth of the Hegemon

Just as there are not two suns in the sky,
so there cannot be two emperors on earth.
—Confucius,
Li ji (Book of Rites), chs. 7, 30;
—Mencius,
Mengzi (Book of Mencius), ch. 5a.4

C hina's "oriental despotism" gave an emperor far more authority than any Western monarch, however absolute. There is
nothing resembling a Magna Carta to be found anywhere in the
long stretch of Chinese history, much less the equivalent of a Greek
Parthenon or a Roman Forum. China moved in the opposite direction, perfecting the early despotism of the Shang and Zhou kings
into the totalitarianism of the Qin, Han, and later dynasties.

Concentrating power in the hands of the sovereign was not
undertaken as an end in itself. Rather it was designed, like the totalitarianism of our own day, to accomplish a larger purpose.
Communist parties wield power in order to crush class opposition and lead the proletariat to communism; emperors wield power
to quell chaos and disorder on earth by establishing hegemony.

Although China's early innovations in statecraft—totalitarianism and hegemony—are less well known than its discovery of gun-
powder or its cultivation of silkworms, they may ultimately prove
to have the greater impact on the world.

China's absolutist traditions go back to the very founding of the
Chinese state.[1] The Shang dynasty (1766?–1027? B.C.), the earliest
for which we have both archaeological and documentary evidence,

was a highly developed state with a tax collection system, a penal code noted for its severity, and—perhaps not unrelated—a standing army. Occupying part of present-day North China, it was ruled by an autocrat who, when addressing his subjects, pointedly styled himself as "I the single one man" [Shang Shu: Pan Geng, Tang shi].

The Shang dynasty was succeeded by the Zhou (1027?– 249 B.C.), which carried on its autocratic traditions. The authority of the King of Zhou over his land and people was absolute, as suggested by a famous passage from the Book of Odes: "All land under heaven belongs to the King, and all people on the shores are subjects of the King" [Shi jing: xiaoya, beishan]. The appellation "Son of Heaven," which has a faintly blasphemous ring to Western ears, was a Zhou invention.

The prerogatives of the Zhou kings, though vast, did not lead initially to complete centralization of power, but rather to Chinese feudalism. To govern the vast expanse of territory under their control, which comprised most of North China, the early Zhou kings enfeoffed kinsmen, bestowing on them limited sovereignty over portions of their domain, along with hereditary titles such as gong (duke), hou (marquis), bo (earl), zi (viscount), and nan (baron). The aristocracy thus created was initially an extended family, with the king heading the main branch of the family tree, while his uncles, brothers, and cousins headed secondary branches. With its decentralized administration—there were 172 feudal domains at the beginning of the Zhou—this Chinese feudalism bore more than a passing resemblance to that found centuries later in Western Europe. The loyalty of Chinese vassals to their king was guaranteed by kinship rather than oath, however, and regulated by the patriarchal kinship law (zong fa) which reserved certain powers to the clan patriarch, who was of course also the king.

With the passage of time the ties that bound the vassals to their king began to fray. Local lords began to regard their fiefs as independent kingdoms. By the end of the eighth century B.C. the Zhou king was no longer able to command the allegiance of the majority of his vassals, nor to maintain order within what had been his domain. From being primus sine paribus he had become merely *primus inter pares.* The King of Zhou's defeat at the hands of the Duke of Zheng in 707 B.C. further reduced him, this time to mere equality with his former vassals.

This removal of central authority at the outset of the Spring and Autumn period (772–481 B.C.) led to a chaotic war "of all against all." According to the *Spring and Autumn Annals (Chunqiu Zuozhuan)*, within a span of two and a half centuries some 483 wars were fought between the scores of feudal states then in existence.

Early in this period it appeared that the large and populous state of Chu, which occupied the middle reaches of the Yangtze River, would quickly emerge victorious. Fear of Chu aggressiveness led the smaller states on the North China plain to turn to the state of Qi, located in modern-day Shandong province, for protection. With a sound economy, a strong military, and an able ruler, Qi was the most respected power in the north. The ruler of Qi, Duke Huan (r. 685–643 B.C.), responded to the appeals of his neighbors by convening a series of conferences beginning in 681 to discuss a common defense against Chu. A mutual defense league was set up, and within three years had grown to include all the central and eastern feudal states. In 678 Duke Huan was officially appointed "Hegemon," or *Ba*, of the league, charged with preserving the peace and defending the honor of the King of Zhou. He did so ably, defending member states from raids by Rong and Yi tribesmen, and keeping Chu at bay throughout his rule.

Duke Huan's success as Hegemon had much to do with a series of political "reforms" initiated by his prime minister, Guan Zhong (?–645 B.C.). With the support of the Duke, Guan Zhong had organized the population along military lines, imposed state regulation on the marketplace, established a state monopoly on coinage, and put the production of salt and iron under state control. Qi's increasingly strong and well-equipped army and its stable and flourishing economy were a direct result of Guan Zhong's reforms, all of which were designed to enhance the authority of the ruler and strengthen the power of the state over society.

Just as Duke Huan was the first Hegemon, so was Guan Zhong

one of the first Legalists, as the school of statecraft dedicated to exalting the ruler and maximizing his power came to be called. According to the *Guan Zi (The Book of Master Guan)*, "The sovereign is the creator of law. The officials are the followers of the law, and the people are the subjects of the law." The ruler must have absolute power to assure his rule. "The wise sovereign holds six powers: to grant life and to kill; to enrich and to impoverish; to promote and to demote" *(Guan Zi*, ch. 45*)*.

The institution of the Hegemon languished after Duke Huan's death, but the revolution in government that he and Guan Zhong had launched continued to spread to other states. Larger and more powerful states, such as Qi, Jin, and Chu, became known as hegemonic powers *(Baquan)* and, undertaking political reforms of their own, began to regulate their populations more closely and maintain standing armies. Smaller and weaker states were conquered and annexed. Only twenty-two states survived to the end of the Spring and Autumn period, the rest having been absorbed by more powerful neighbors.[2] The "foreign policy" of these states could be summed up in a single word: conquest.

This struggle intensified during the aptly named Warring States period which followed. The key to survival lay in organization and aggressiveness, in building large standing armies, and in using these to conquer as much territory and as many subjects as possible. The strong states originally numbered twelve, but as one state after another fell victim to conquest this number was reduced to seven. This process, as had long been obvious, could have only one end: the creation of a single state, ruled by an omnipotent ruler, holding all power under heaven.

The rulers of the Seven Powers, who now styled themselves "kings," deliberately set about to concentrate as much power in their hands as possible, putting their individual countries virtually on a full-time war footing. In this they were assisted by councilors collectively known as the Legalists, whose governing slogan was to "enrich the state and strengthen the military" *[fuguo qiangbing].*[3] The *Zeitgeist* of the late Zhou is best expressed by the greatest Legalist, Han Fei, who variously remarked that "Today the competition depends on having the greatest force," and "He who has great force will be paid tribute by others, he who has less force will pay tribute to others; therefore the wise ruler cultivates force."[4]

Han Fei and other Legalists helped to design and implement a series of political "reforms" to enhance the authority of the monarch, to build and maintain a strong army, to increase agricultural production, to build up an appointed bureaucracy (replacing an unreliable hereditary aristocracy), to increase state revenues, to improve the state's ability to regulate commerce, to intimidate the people into subjection, and to crush any and all dissent. The "totalitarian regulation of society in the service of the state" is how Sinologist Charles Hucker has described the Legalist program.[5]

The essence of Legalist doctrines was the supremacy of the ruler: "The ruler occupies the position of power dominating over the people and commands the wealth of the state." (Han Fei Zi, ch. 14) In order to concentrate power in the hands of the ruler, the Legalist program consciously set out to weaken the nobility and further subjugate the common people.[6]

To strengthen the state at the expense of the nobility, the Legalists advised their sovereigns that they should no longer share power with a class of hereditary feudal lords. Within the court, aristocratic officials serving in inherited posts found themselves replaced by appointed bureaucrats, often ordinary gentry-scholars or non-natives, whom the ruler could discharge, or even execute, at will.[7] In the countryside, likewise, feudal lords were displaced by appointed magistrates who served at the pleasure of the ruler. Their inherited fiefs were redrawn into administrative units called counties (xian). By appointing officials who were mere extensions of themselves, Chinese rulers crushed the nobility and gathered yet more power into their hands.

To strengthen the ruler's hand over the people, the Legalists recommended such policies as:

- accumulation of people as an indispensable component of power: "Therefore the ruler of men desires to have more people for his own use. . . . The ruler loves the people because they are useful." (Guan Zi, ch. 16)

- suppression of all voluntary associations: "The early kings always made certain that the interests of their subjects diverged. Thus under perfect governance, spouses and friends, however close to one another, can neither refuse to report another's crimes, nor cover up for them." *(Shangjun shu,* ch. 24; also *Han Fei Zi,* ch. 45)
- establishment of informer networks: "The wise ruler forces the whole world to hear and to watch for him. . . . No one in the world can hide from him or scheme against him." *(Han Fei Zi,* ch. 14)
- use of punishment instead of reward: "A well-governed state . . . employs nine punishments to one reward; whereas a weak state employs nine rewards to one punishment." *(Shangjun shu,* ch. 7)
- harsh punishment for violations according to set laws: "If crimes are punished by execution, then the law wins over the people and the army is strong. *(Shangjun shu,* ch. 5)
- mutual surveillance and collective punishment: "The people were commanded to be organized into groups of fives and tens. They must be under mutual surveillance and punished for crimes committed by other members of their group. Those who failed to inform against a crime were to be cut in half at the waist." *(Shi ji,* ch. 68)

The advice of these Chinese Machiavellis grates cynically, even immorally, on Western ears, but it found ready listeners among the dwindling ranks of Chinese kings. By the closing century of the Warring States period it was clear that all but one of them would be destroyed. Which of them could resist the additional power promised by the Legalists, not just for its own sake, but in order to strike at the others? Who among them did not want to become Hegemon and rule over the known world?

Most of these kings embarked upon the Legalist "reforms," carrying out within their territories what Professor Zhengyuan Fu calls a "revolution from above." The Chinese people seem to have put up little resistance against this regimentation, perhaps because five centuries of incessant warfare had left them prostrate, or perhaps because they saw security in the imposition of a rigid Legalist order. This formative period of Chinese history left deep scars on the Chinese mind, which ever after has been prone to an irrational fear of "chaos" and "disorder."

As the Legalist reforms took hold, a cynical absolutism became entrenched in state after state. But it was the kingdom of Qin in the west, under the direction of the great Legalist Shang Yang, that took the most drastic measures to eliminate feudalism, centralize political power, and militarize. The result was the transformation of the Qin state from a backward dukedom to the leading—and most brutal—power in North China.

When the Shanxi state of Zhao fell to the Qin in 260 B.C., the entire surrendered Zhao army of some 400,000 men was butchered. The Qin annexed the territory of the last Zhou king in 256 B.C., and then absorbed the last remaining states during a ten-year campaign beginning in 231 B.C. It was through the ensuing Qin dynasty that the absolutism embodied in the Legalist reforms became embedded in Chinese political culture, to be practiced down to the present day.

THE QIN DYNASTY: A MODEL FOR SUBSEQUENT DYNASTIES

Prior to the Warring States period, Chinese peasants could go about their daily lives largely unmolested by the government except for taxes and occasional stints of corvée labor. However despotic the ruler who sat on the local dragon throne, however much he terrorized his courtiers at his capital and his kinsmen in neighboring fiefs, off in the villages a kind of grassroots autonomy flourished. Peasants summed up their freedom from overbearing government in a folk saying: "Heaven is high and the emperor is far away."

Even before his final triumph over his fellow kings, the First Emperor of the Qin had lessened the distance between himself and his subjects by means of Legalist reforms. Now he sought to eliminate it altogether. During an age when the reach of even the most ambitious rulers almost always exceeded their grasp, the Qin emperor sought to make the entire population of China, at the time some forty million people, directly accountable to him. Acting through an enormous cadre of bureaucrats, a complex network of laws, and a highly elaborated ideology, he very largely succeeded. In so doing, the Qin emperor became the archetype for a political monster that has become all too common in our modern age. More than two millennia before George Orwell coined the term, ancient China endured the world's first Big Brother.

Qin Shihuang is a household name throughout the Orient, yet few in the West, outside of a handful of Orientalists, have heard of this grandfather of all despots. Blessed with a vigorous constitution, and assisted by the ruthless Legalist Li Si, he threw all of his energies into the quest for power. In 231 B.C. he launched the series of campaigns that, within ten years, would bring much of what constitutes modern China into his domain, creating the largest empire the world had known up to that time. For the next twelve years, until his death in 210 B.C., he ruled with an iron hand.

But it was not so much his personality as his policies, crafted in conjunction with Li Si, that so stunningly anticipated the bureaucratic totalitarian empires of our own century. To begin with, a special cadre of commissars was established to keep watch over officialdom. At the provincial level, for example, there was a civil governor, a military commander, and a political commissar. The duties of the commissar were, like their latter-day counterparts in Communist countries, to spy on the governor and military commander and ensure that they did not deviate from the official line or criticize government policy. All civil and military officials were centrally appointed and salaried, and they served at the pleasure of the emperor.

The emperor's Legalist credo was that "a wise prince doesn't ask his subjects to behave well—he uses methods that prevent them from behaving badly." Every arena of life was to be regulated. The people were not permitted to bear arms, and all weapons were confiscated and sent to the capital. Aristocratic families were uprooted from their estates and moved en masse to the capital. Trade was viewed as "parasitical activity" and made illegal. Wandering minstrels were banned and replaced by authorized troupes of singers and musicians whose repertories had to be approved by the Ministry of the Interior.

As laws proliferated, the bureaucracies charged with enforcing them fattened. Fierce punishments calculated to squelch any murmur of resistance were meted out to violators. For major capital crimes, not only the offender but his entire family was annihilated. Those convicted of lesser crimes were sent by the millions to labor on government projects in a forerunner of the modern-day gulag. For the construction of the Emperor Qin Shihuang's palace, for example, more than seven hundred thousand laborers were conscripted, while for the construction of his tomb a similar number were drafted. (Shi ji, ch. 6) Hundreds of thousands more labored to build some 4,000 miles of imperial highways, as many as were built by the Roman Empire. Countless others dug canals and widened waterways to allow water transport for the 1,200 miles from the Yangtse to Guangzhou. Others were sent north to strengthen the walls that earlier Chinese states had built.[8]

Yet the lesson of the Warring States period was that safety lies not behind defensive walls, but in a policy of aggressive expansion. Qin Shihuang had risen to power by practicing such a policy, and this policy he continued. The Qin emperor launched a series of wars to subjugate neighboring peoples and expand the borders of the nation. Armies were sent campaigning southward against the Yue people, the ancestors of the present-day Vietnamese, whose coastal state then stretched up to modern-day Guangdong. The campaign was long and difficult because the Yue adopted guerrilla tactics, avoiding pitched battles in favor of raids on outlying Qin towns and garrisons. Still, much of southeastern China was brought within the Qin domain, with Qin outposts stretching down to the Hanoi area of present-day Vietnam. Armies were sent northward into Inner Mongolia as well, in an effort to drive back the Xiongnu confederation, although the mobility of these nomadic herdsmen made them difficult to subdue permanently.

To concentrate the state power needed to carry out these hegemonic thrusts, the world's first cult of personality was invented. Clever ministers attributed godlike powers to the Qin emperor, and official bards spread stories of his fabulous accomplishments throughout the length and breadth of the empire. One minister had giant footprints four feet long and two feet wide carved in the rock of a sacred mountain, and let it be known that these had been made by the august emperor's shoes. At the summit of another sacred mountain another minister placed a set of chess pieces as tall as a man. The emperor, he avowed, had ascended the mountain and played chess with the gods. Everywhere steles were raised with deeply carved inscriptions lauding the emperor and the accomplishments of his rule. "All men under the sun work with one heart," these read in part. "Morals have been standardized. Neighbors keep watch on one another, relatives inform on relatives, and thieves lie low!" Few among his fearful subjects dared disobey the Qin emperor's edicts.

Still, despite the harshness of his laws and the strength of his personality cult, occasional acts of sedition did occur. The only way to achieve perfect control over his subjects, Li Si informed the emperor, was to eradicate thought itself. "Your Majesty . . . has firmly established for yourself a position of sole supremacy. . . . And yet these independent schools [Confucianists and others], joining with each other, criticize the codes of laws and instructions. Hearing of the promulgation of a decree, they criticize it, each from the standpoint of his own school. At home they disapprove of it in their hearts; going out they criticize it in the thoroughfare. They seek a reputation by discrediting their sovereign; they appear superior by expressing contrary views, and they lead the lowly multitude in the spreading of slander. If such license is not prohibited, the sovereign power will decline above and partisan factions will form below. It would be well to prohibit this. Your servant suggests that all books in the imperial archives, save the memoirs of Qin, be burned."[9]

Qin Shihuang agreed, and issued an imperial edict:

> Anyone owning classical books or treatises on philosophy must hand them in within thirty days. After thirty days anyone found in possession of such writings will be branded on the cheek and sent to work as a laborer on the northern wall

or some other government project. The only exceptions are books on medicine, drugs, astrology, and agronomy.

Private schools will be forbidden. Those who wish to study law will do so under government officials.

Anyone indulging in political or philosophical discussion will be put to death, and his body exposed in public.

Scholars who use examples from antiquity to criticize the present, or who praise early dynasties in order to throw doubt on the policies of our own, most enlightened sovereign, will be executed, they and their families!

Government officials who turn a blind eye to the above-mentioned crimes will be deemed guilty by virtue of the principle of collective responsibility, and will incur the same punishment as that inflicted for the offense itself.

The consequences of the edict were swift and devastating. Pyres of burning books lit up the cities and towns as China's ancient literature was reduced to ashes. For possessing forbidden texts, three million men had their faces branded with the stamp of infamy and were deported to the Great Wall. Numerous scholars committed suicide in protest, while others hanged or drowned themselves out of fear.

It is for his punishment of 463 famous Confucian scholars that the Qin emperor is most notorious. These were individuals that the Qin emperor personally tried and found guilty of conspiracy, sabotage, and lese-majesty. In the supreme atrocity of a long record of Qin brutality, he sentenced them to the five tortures: beating, amputation of the nose, branding of the cheek, amputation of the feet, and castration. Then they were buried up to their necks in the earth and their heads crushed by chariot wheels.[10]

Ordinary people were treated as a disposable resource of the state. The terra cotta soldiers discovered near China's ancient capital of Changan may have survived far longer than the bones of those construction workers buried alive to hide the location of the tomb from grave robbers, but it is those old bones of real victims—not the terra cotta soldiers—that express the early history of China's superordination of state over society.[11]

The ruthlessness of the Qin state led to a widespread and smoldering resentment, which flared up into open rebellion upon the emperor's death. The insurrection began when a few hundred peas-ant conscripts were delayed by inclement weather from reporting in to the authorities at the appointed time and place. Knowing the harsh punishment that awaited such tardiness, they decided to become rebels instead. Armed only with wooden sticks, they began a guerrilla war against the government. Within three years the whole imposing edifice of the Qin collapsed into ruin.

Although the Qin dynasty did not survive the death of its founder, the Legalist concept of "revolution from above" had trans-formed China forever. Warring states had been welded together into an empire. The aristocracy had been replaced by a bureaucracy. Power had been centralized into the hands of a Son of Heaven. The autocratic political system that the Qing designed—with its absolute monarch, centralized bureaucracy, state domination over society, law as a penal tool of the ruler, mutual surveillance and informer network, persecution of dissidents, and political practices of coercion and intimidation—entered China's cultural DNA and continued to replicate itself down through the centuries and the dynasties. It is little surprise that China remains a centralized, auto-cratic, bureaucratic government—and empire-in-waiting—even today.

"CONFUCIANIST ON THE OUTSIDE, LEGALIST ON THE INSIDE"

The fall of the Qin dynasty exposed both the strengths and weak-nesses of the Legalist approach. On the positive side of the ledger, Legalism had proven admirably suited for the education of ambi-tious rulers. Acting on the Legalists' frank, brutal, and cynical advice, China's first emperor had created the world's first totali-tarian state. At the same time, in arguing that authority rests on naked force alone, and that the chief instrument of effective gov-ernment is raw terror, the Legalists had seriously misjudged human nature. For while it is possible to terrorize a people into submis-sion, the risks of such a policy are not only sullen resistance but even open rebellion. Human beings respond far more readily to commands issuing from an authority they recognize as legitimate, than those from one they fear. The Legalists had been so busy telling the people they *must* obey their rulers, that they had never gotten around to telling them why they *should.*

The emperors of the succeeding dynasty, the Han, were determined to avoid making the same mistake. Their dynasty would only survive, they realized, if they balanced Legalist intimidation with Confucian indoctrination. Had not Confucius taught that one of a ruler's most important responsibilities was to educate his subjects in virtue through exhortation, persuasion and, above all, moral example? "If a ruler himself is upright, all will go well without command. If the ruler himself is not upright, even when he gives commands, he will not be obeyed." *(Lun yu,* ch. 13.6) Or again: "He who exercises government by means of his virtue may be compared to the North Star, which keeps its place and all stars turn towards it." *(Lun yu,* ch. 2.1)

The chief Confucian value that rulers were to exemplify and teach their people was *ren,* which has been variously translated into English as benevolence, humaneness, virtue, compassion, and goodness. Confucius defined *ren* variously as "love of mankind" *(Lun yu,* ch. 12.22); "humility, tolerance, good faith, diligence and kindness" *(Lun yu,* ch. 17.6); and the precept "do not do unto others what you do not want others to do unto you" *(Lun yu,* chs. 15.23, 12.2).

Yet although their worldviews may seem far apart, the Confucians and the Legalists were not really in disagreement on the structure of authority. Both saw the world as properly consisting of a single unified state *(tian xia)* under the centralized political authority of a single, all-powerful sovereign: "Just as there are not two suns in the sky, so there cannot be two emperors on earth." (Confucius, *Li ji,* chs. 7, 30; Mencius, *Mengzi,* ch. 5a.4) Both saw the people in a posture of absolute submission towards this emperor. The difference was that while the Legalists knocked heads, the Confucians taught respect for authority—and the people kowtowed of their own accord.

Confucianism was so well suited to the task of persuading the people to become compliant subjects that in 136 B.C. the Emperor Han Wudi declared it to be the official ideology of the empire.

Not that he or his successors were themselves true believers in this new state religion. Far from it. Even though the occupants of the imperial throne thereafter made a great show of celebrating Confucianism and its rites in public, they were "Confucianist on the outside, Legalist on the inside" *(wairu neifa).* For cynical and sophisticated Legalist rulers, Confucianism was merely a secret force to police the mind far more thoroughly than cadres of informers ever could.

This duality was not always a tightly guarded secret. Emperor Han Xuandi (r. 73–49 B.C.), for instance, was open about his family's continued appreciation of Legalism as well as its disdain for the impracticalities of Confucianism: "The Han family dynasty has its own institution. It is a blending of the Way of the Hegemon [i.e. Legalism] with that of the Sage-King [i.e. Confucianism]. How can we rely solely on the teaching of benevolence and apply the political rules of the Zhou dynasty [i.e. Confucianism]? The vulgar Confucians do not understand the expediencies of changing times. They like to praise the ancients and criticize the present. They confuse the people concerning what is nominal and what is real, and they do not know what to abide by. How can they be entrusted with responsibility?" *(Han shu, ch. 9)*

Given such sentiments, it is not surprising that the ancient Confucian texts—*The Analects of Confucius, The Great Learning, The Doctrine of the Mean,* and *The Works of Mencius*—were rewritten over the course of the Han dynasty to make them better serve the cause of imperial autocracy.[12] Confucius is made to express Legalist and Daoist beliefs entirely foreign to his thinking. This inveterate defender of the Golden Age of Chinese antiquity is compelled to condemn it in the manner of a Legalist: "If a man living in the present age returns to the ways of antiquity, disaster will certainly befall him." *(Zhongyong, ch. 29)* Or he is made to utter the un-Confucian idea that the ruler, not antiquity, is the only sure guide to proper behavior: "No one but the Son of Heaven may order the ceremonies, establish standards, and determine the written characters." *(Zhongyong, ch. 29)* Or, to invoke the Way of the Daoists to suppress dissent: "When the Way prevails, the common people do not discuss public affairs." *(Lun yu, ch. 16.2)*[13]

The stolen prestige of China's great sage and of the (newly reconstructed) Confucian classics were cynically used to legitimate Legalist rule and practice. Few emperors made more than a show of following that benevolent Way preached by Confucius, although they all justified their policies as being "for the good of the people." As Professor Zhengyuan Fu writes, "the Confucian text provided ready-made and convincing propaganda for ideological legitimation of authority no matter what kind of person the ruler might be, rationalization of policy no matter what consequences it would result in, and justification of political practice no matter how repressive it really was."[14] Confucian paternalism had become little more than a pleasant mask worn by the emperors to hide the Legalistic totalitarianism that lay at the heart of Chinese despotism.[15]

EMPIRE WITHOUT BOUNDARIES

If the internal policy of the Hegemon is oppression and thought control, what is his foreign policy? Strictly speaking, the Hegemon has no foreign policy other than one of continuous aggression against and absorption of neighboring states. Hegemony is like a crystal which, in the proper medium, continues to replicate its existing structure indefinitely. Other states, by their very existence, challenge the principle of hegemony. Perfect hegemony would have no external expression at all, because it would have brought all neighboring states and peoples under its crystalline control.

The first goal of the aspiring Hegemon in Chinese history was the unification of the 1.5 million square miles of China Proper—roughly the eastern half of present-day China.[16] But the desire for hegemony which drove him to these early conquests did not expire when these boundaries were reached. Armed with the manpower and resources provided by the conquest of China Proper, the ambitious Hegemon went on to incorporate another one to two million square miles into his imperial realm. In the end, the relatively primitive means of transportation and communication he was forced to rely upon dictated the outer limits of the territory under his direct control. Beyond this point, the hegemonic imperative found expression not in conquest but in compelling outlying territories to acknowledge the Hegemon as vassal or tributary states. In this way the Chinese Hegemon almost always sought to rule his known world. And almost always succeeded.

At times of dynastic expansion, China has dominated much more territory than it controls today. Its greatest expansion took place under the Mongols, when its empire stretched from the Bering Sea all the way to the gates of Warsaw. At its greatest extent the Mongol Empire dominated an area remarkably similar in scope to the Sino-Soviet bloc. Even during less tumescent dynastic expansions China remained, for most of human history, the world's leading power.

The greatest empire of the ancient Western world was governed from Rome. It reached its maximum territorial extent in A.D. 211, when it exercised control over the entire shoreline of the Mediterranean Sea, most of the Black Sea, and England. It had a polyglot population of some sixty million souls and a standing army of perhaps 350,000. In addition to the Praetorian Guard, thirty legions of 10,000 men were deployed abroad, garrisoning the frontier provinces and border states.[17]

Yet to the east a greater empire had already been in existence for over four hundred years. By the time of Christ, the Han dynasty also governed no fewer than sixty million souls. Dating from 202 B.C., the Han Empire was more impressive in scope and organization than the contemporaneous Roman Empire. Its sway extended from Korea eastward across Mongolia to Central Asia, and included most of contemporary China except Hainan Island and Tibet. It possessed a standing army of over a million men.[18]

In a pattern that was to be repeated again and again throughout Chinese history, with unification came foreign conquests. During the long and brilliant reign of Han Wudi (140–87 B.C.), Han armies marched to all points of the compass. In the northeast they conquered the Korean peninsula. In the south they brought all of what is now South China under their control, and carried their arms as far southward as the Gulf of Tonkin, in present-day Vietnam. Their major effort was directed against the northwest "barbarians," especially the Xiongnu. Alliances against this common foe were made with central Asiatic peoples. To coordinate the alliances an official named Zhang Qian was sent to the west and went as far as Bactria, or modern-day Kyrgyzstan. The power of the Xiongnu was broken and the Han rule was extended into what is now Xinjiang. The remains of fortresses and walls built by the Han to guard their frontier in the far northwest can still be seen today.

The first century of the Christian era saw further Han conquests in the west. Under General Ban Zhao the Chinese became masters of parts of central Asia. Their armies reached the shores of the Caspian Sea in A.D. 97, and a Chinese embassy was sent to the Persian Gulf. Partly because of the control by the Han of the caravan routes to central Asia and partly because of the possession of Tonkin and the south, commerce was maintained with the Roman orient—known to the Chinese as Dacin (Da Qin)—both by land and by sea. Chinese silks were carried to the Mediterranean world, while products from central Asia and the Hellenistic world were brought to China.

Although Han dynasty China may not have surpassed ancient Rome in population, it exercised a more direct control over that population through a civil service, the first the world had ever known. While Rome ruled through military governors, consuls and proconsuls, as well as through the heads of vassal states, the Han emperor ruled directly through civil officials personally appointed by the occupant of the Dragon Throne. The Chinese empire was a more intricate financial, economic, and security organization than the Roman, not merely because of its greater size, but because of its greater complexity.

The aspiration of elites among the various peoples who lived under the Roman Eagle was to be able to say *Civis Romanus sum*, "I am a Roman citizen"—that is, to be formally admitted into the Roman polity, with all the rights and duties that such inclusion implied. By this means the upper social strata of many peoples along the Mediterranean littoral were partly assimilated into Roman culture, adopting Roman dress and speaking Latin, at least in dealings with the state. Rome's cultural superiority reinforced its imperial power and gave it a tremendous advantage over the polyglot, multicultural empires common in other parts of the world, where rule by brute force remained the norm.

In China this process of assimilation, for various reasons, went much deeper. The assurance of cultural superiority was not only a matter of subjective arrogance on the part of the Chinese elite, but a perspective shared by other peoples within China's expanding shadow. The superiority of the Chinese way of life, with its advanced agriculture, its written language, and its highly developed arts, was so attractive that those who fell under Chinese rule often came to admire their conquerors greatly and actively seek to assimilate. This cultural superiority was augmented by the combination of Confucian ritual, stressing harmony, hierarchy and discipline, with the calculated ruthlessness of Legalist rulers. Unlike the states absorbed into the Roman Empire, where assimilation occurred mainly at the top, whole peoples conquered by the Hegemon quickly redefined themselves as Chinese, adopted Chinese language, dress and agricultural practices, and disappeared without a trace into the Chinese sea. More than conquered, they were thoroughly Sinicized. Ancient Chinese texts make many references to peoples who long ago ceased to exist as separate ethnic groups, so completely have they been assimilated into Chinese culture.

Civil officials replaced military governors within a generation or two, as the identity of the conquered peoples merged with that of the conquerors. China's unity became not merely the artificial construct of military force or the nominal allegiance of elites, as in the Roman Empire, but something rooted in a deeply held and popular desire. It was reinforced by the civil service, professionally trained and competitively recruited, and by rigid Legalist controls on public and private activities.

Cultural homogeneity enabled the Han dynasty to last for some 360 years. Even more importantly, it enabled China, after a period of division into three Chinese states, to recoalesce into the Sui-Tang dynasty in A.D. 589. The Roman Empire, less culturally cohesive, had split into eastern and western empires in A.D. 412 and continued to wane, the latter soon ceasing to exist. China, on the other hand, has gone through successive cycles of unification and fragmentation right up to the present day, with the centripetal forces of language and culture overcoming again and again the centrifugal forces of decay and deterioration.

At each dynastic recrudescence, China became once again the largest and most powerful empire on earth. And with each reassertion of unity came foreign conquest. During the early decades of the Sui-Tang dynasty (589–906),[19] border territories that had been lost, such as Korea and Xinjiang, were recaptured. Then Chinese armies struck to the southwest and entered Tibet, eventually crossing the Pamirs into northwest India. At one point even Persia sought and received aid from the Tang against the Moslem Arab wave of invasion. The Song (960–1279) saw similar exploits in its early years.

The period of China's greatest imperial expansion came during the Yuan dynasty (1260–1368), when the empire included all Asia north of the Himalayas except Japan, and reached to the heart of Europe. From his capital of Khanbaliq, near the site of modern-day Beijing, Kublai Khan ruled not only over China but over most of the Mongol Empire, with its western frontiers in Mesopotamia and Europe. Armies were sent into Champa, Annan and Burma, and armadas against Java and Japan. The expeditions to the south ended in a somewhat inglorious retirement, the attempt on Java was unsuccessful, and the armada against Japan was destroyed by a typhoon. Still, for a time much of the Eurasian land mass was ruled from a Chinese capital. It may be argued that it was Mongolian mobility and tactics that created the largest empire the world had ever known, but it is equally true that its center of gravity was China, which provided strength, stability and, increasingly, a sense of purpose. Not for the last time, barbarians from the north provided the military means to achieve in China and beyond the paramount end of power: hegemony.

The Ming dynasty (1368–1644), which followed, is often described as inward-looking, but its early history recapitulates that of its predecessors. The founder of the Ming dynasty, Hong Wu, managed to oust the Mongols and keep China from fragmenting. An outgrowth of this continued unity was conquest. Hong Wu sent expeditions to the south and southeast as far as Java and Ceylon.

One of the princes of Ceylon was brought captive to China, and for years tribute came from the island. Under a succeeding monarch an expedition was sent by sea as far as the Persian Gulf. Under the Ming emperors, Korea was invaded, Annan for a time became subject to China, and frequent wars with the Mongols kept those ancient enemies beyond the wall.

The Qing, like its predecessors, was held together by an exquisitely organized mandarinate, whose members were selected by competitive examinations and represented the best and brightest of the Chinese elite. The Qing rulers also instituted the same rigid Legalist controls over society as previous dynasties. Scholar-officials could not meet in groups of more than ten without official approval, books were subject to rigorous censorship, newspapers were unknown, school curricula were controlled, and independent voluntary associations were strongly discouraged, if not absolutely forbidden. "No private undertaking nor any aspect of public life could escape official regulation," observes French Sinologist Etienne Balazs.[20] Civil society—that part of the social system that is not under the control of the state—was largely unknown and ideological unity was strictly enforced.

Under the able leadership of Kangxi (1662–1722) and Qianlong (1736–96), a prosperous China went on the march. Qing armies conquered Manchuria and Mongolia. Under Kangxi they added Tibet and Formosa to their possessions. Under Qianlong, Ili and Turkestan came under Chinese rule. Qianlong's legions penetrated Burma, Nepal and Annan. Korea paid tribute.

The Qing dynasty circa 1800 was an impressive assertion of hegemony. The imperial center directly ruled a vast territory stretching from the Russian Far East across southern Siberia to Lake Balkash, southward across Kazakhstan, and eastward along the Himalayas, Laos, and Vietnam. Through vassal and tributary states it controlled Burma, Nepal, Indochina, Thailand, and Korea. More than 300 million people lived within the Celestial Empire, while tens of millions more resided in surrounding tributary states. The economy was the world's largest and the military, although beginning to fall behind the West in technological innovations, was still impressive in numbers.

One of the lessons of this glorious history, a lesson deeply etched in the minds of Chinese students today, is that each of China's empires—the Han, the Sui-Tang, the Song, the Yuan, the Ming and the Qing—had no contemporary peer. No other power of comparable might existed in the world. Few of China's neighbors proved capable of resisting her determined expansion. The reigning Chinese Hegemon projected power almost at will over his periphery, constrained at times by hostile powers but more commonly only by his own whims.

For over two thousand years the Middle Kingdom was the center of the universe, a huge, self-satisfied continent of people whose elite, wealthy and cultured, had only disdain for the barbarians living on its periphery. Smugly convinced of their country's cultural and military superiority, China's leaders wanted little from the rest of the world except its deference.

In 1792, King George III thought to entice China into a trading relationship by sending emissaries bearing gifts of British manufactured goods. Whatever modest goodwill this gesture may have won was dissipated when the British refused to kowtow to the emperor. His imperial majesty, deeply offended by this lack of due deference, sent them packing. The edict of their expulsion reveals the invincible self-confidence that would remain embedded in China's cultural marrow in the centuries ahead: "We, by the Grace of Heaven, Emperor, instruct the King of England to take note of our charge: The Celestial Empire, ruling all within the four seas . . . does not value rare and precious things . . . nor do we have the slightest need of your country's manufactures. . . . Hence we . . . have commanded your tribute envoys to return safely home. You, O King, should simply act in conformity with our wishes by strengthening your loyalty and swearing perpetual obedience."

But the Empire was already fraying at the edges by the time Emperor Kangxi so haughtily dismissed the English envoys, and within a few decades it would be defeated by Great Britain in the Opium War of 1839–42. For China this was more than just a military defeat. It was a profound cultural humiliation. The deeply

ingrained sense of superiority, inculcated over millennia of dominating their near neighbors, stood revealed as hollow pride. The
demeaning political realities of the past hundred years, which have
sometimes caused the Chinese to look back at their glorious past
and wonder if they were merely dwarves standing on the shoulders
of giants, have only deepened the insult.

CHAPTER THREE

The Hegemon Reawakens

M ao Zedong announced the founding of the People's Republic of China on October 1,1949, in words that look back on the glorious past in terms of wounded national pride:

> The Chinese have always been a great, courageous and industrious nation; it is only in modern times that they have fallen behind. And that was due entirely to oppression and exploitation by foreign imperialism and domestic reactionary governments. . . . Ours will no longer be a nation subject to insult and humiliation. We have stood up.

The old Hegemon had awakened from its slumber and would soon set out upon the same well-traveled road it had traversed so many times before. In the view of China's Communist elite, a cabal of Western and Western-oriented countries—Russia, Great Britain, France, Germany, Japan and America—had treacherously combined to attack the old Chinese empire, loosening China's grip on hundreds of thousands of square miles of territory and a dozen tributary states in the process.

Mao reserved special rancor for the United States, fulminating in a bitterly sarcastic speech called "'Friendship' or Aggression" in late 1949:

> The history of the aggression against China by U.S. imperialism, from 1840 when it helped the British in the Opium War to the time it was thrown out of China by the Chinese people, should be written into a concise textbook for the education of Chinese youth. The United States was one of the first countries to force China to cede extraterritoriality. . . . All the 'friendship' shown to China by U.S. imperialism over the past

109 years, and especially the great act of 'friendship' in helping Chiang Kai-shek slaughter several million Chinese the last
few years—all this had one purpose [according to the
Americans] . . . first, to maintain the Open Door, second, to
respect the administrative and territorial integrity of China
and, third, to oppose any foreign domination of China. Today,
the only doors still open to [U.S. Secretary of State] Acheson
and his like are in small strips of land, such as Canton and
Taiwan.[1]

FIRST EMPEROR OF THE MAO DYNASTY

Mao Zedong, who was at least as well versed in Chinese history
as in Marxist dialectics, envisioned himself as much the founding emperor of a new dynasty as the ruler of a communist state.
His poem "White Snow," written in 1936, scarcely cloaks his vaunt-
ing ambition:

How beautiful these mountains and rivers,
enticing countless heroes to war and strife.
Too bad that Emperors Qin Shihuang and Han Wudi
lacked culture and that Emperors Tang Taizong and
Song Taizu lacked romance.
Genghis Khan was the pride of his time,
though he was only good at shooting eagles with his bow.
They all belong to a time gone by.
Only today is a True Hero present.[2]

The True Hero was proposing himself, correctly as it worked
out, to be superior in both ability and ruthlessness to other dynastic founders. If he was offended by comparisons that many made
between himself and Emperor Qin Shihuang, arguably the most
hated figure in Chinese history, it was only because he saw himself as Emperor Qin's superior in ruthlessness and cunning. At
the Second Plenum of the Eighth Party Congress in May 1958, Mao
scoffed, "Emperor Qin Shihuang was not that outstanding. He only
buried alive 460 Confucian scholars. We buried 460 *thousand*
Confucian scholars. [Some democratic personages] have accused us
of being Emperor Qin Shihuang. This is not true [I told them].
We are a hundred times worse than Emperor Qin. To the charge
of being like Emperor Qin, of being a dictator, we plead guilty.

But you have not said nearly enough [I told them], for often we have to go further [than Emperor Qin Shihuang did]."[3]

In another of his poems, Mao contrasted his admiration for Emperor Qin Shihuang and the Legalist order to his utter disdain for Confucius:

> Please don't slander Emperor Qin Shihuang, Sir,
> for the burning of the books should be thought through again.
> Our ancestral dragon, though dead, lives on in spirit,
> while Confucius, though renowned, was really rubbish.
> The Qin order has survived from age to age. . . .

Mao's disdain for Confucianism was rooted less in his Marxist-Leninism than in his Legalism. Like the Legalist Emperor Han Xuandi quoted in the previous chapter, Mao despised the old Confucian orthodoxy for its impracticalities, for its moral niceties, for its preachiness about virtue and benevolence. Even more, he despised it because its tottering remains stood in the way of building a strong state that would dominate the Chinese and neighboring peoples.

Growing up around the turn of the twentieth century, Mao had steeped himself in Chinese historical classics, absorbing the frank and brutal Legalist advice they offered to would-be hegemons.[4] His ambition was to found a dynasty by naked force, to be a new Emperor Qin Shihuang, to rule all of China's traditional domains through the same kind of totalitarian institutions. To successfully establish the "Qin order" in the modern age, however, he needed a replacement for Confucianism, a new legitimating ideology that the people could be taught. He needed to reconfigure Legalism for modern times.

With the victory of the communist revolution in Russia, Mao and the rest of China's revolutionaries found an unlikely companion for their authoritarian ambitions: an imported Marxist ideology that was every bit as statist and elitist as traditional Chinese political culture, while at the same time claiming to be even more "modern" and "progressive" than its chief ideological opponent, liberal democracy.

Democracy, after all, was the nemesis of the Hegemon, dispersing power among elected representatives instead of concentrating it in the hands of the ruler, weakening instead of strengthening the state, empowering rather than subjugating the people. The principle of the self-determination of peoples, in particular, threatened to undermine hegemony by opening the possibility that border regions where minorities were numerically dominant, such as Tibet and Xinjiang, would go their own way.

While formally acknowledging civil rights and the equality of man, Marxist-Leninism was an enabler for the Hegemon. It defended the monopoly of power by an educated elite, and defined a relationship between state and society very much in keeping with China's autocratic tradition. It was a much more effective tool of indoctrination than Confucianism and, with its pseudoscientific terminology, provided a stronger defense for autocratic rule. As a bonus, it even commanded a respectful audience in the very heart of Western society.

Communism was, in fact, an allegory for hegemony, showing how the revolution that had come to China was predestined to spread to neighboring countries. Meanwhile, China could keep a tight grip on border regions; it would only be a matter of time until a common proletarian identity unified China's diverse ethnic nationalities. For Chinese intellectuals uncomfortable with the radical individualism underlying Western values and fearful that the weakening, even the dissolution, of China would result from them, "scientific" Marxist-Leninism proved a powerful magnet, drawing thousands of them into the Chinese Communist Party.

For the illiterate or semiliterate villagers who became the foot soldiers of Mao's armies, the principles of liberal democracy were unknown and the abstractions of Marxist-Leninist ideology a mystery. But simple resonance with dynastic China's Confucian beliefs and imperial traditions helped to make communism and its leader acceptable. Dialectics argued for change just as did the yin-yang theory and the *Book of Change*. The state remained the grand provider on whom all relied for their survival. The paternalistic party as the vanguard of the proletariat was understood as a stand-in for the "father-mother officialdom" of imperial times. The paramount leader was the omnipotent savior upon whose benevolent rule all subjects depended.

Mao's "personality cult" was already flourishing by April 1945, when the new Party Constitution declared the "Thought of Mao Zedong" essential to "guide the entire work" of the Party. The chairman was praised as "not only the greatest revolutionary and statesman in Chinese history but also the greatest theoretician and scientist." As always, much of this fulsome praise came from Mao's own hand.[5]

Most importantly, the cult of the Party chairman was seen as a continuation of the cult of the emperor. The party went to extraordinary lengths to prey upon the superstitions of the people in this regard. Mao was endlessly exalted as a larger-than-life figure, a kind of living god who would rescue the people from oppression. As soon as the Communists captured a village in the civil war, its buildings would blossom with slogans like "Mao Zedong is the great savior of the Chinese people."

As for Mao himself, he may have served communism, but only because it served him. If the emperors had been "Confucianist on the outside, Legalist on the inside," then Mao was effectively "Communist on the outside, Legalist on the inside." As cynical and sophisticated as the most ruthless Legalist rulers, he took full advantage of China's millennia-long totalitarian tradition to consolidate his rule. A study of references and quotations in Mao's *Selected Works* is revealing: some 24 percent came from Stalin, the most ruthless Soviet leader of all time; but almost as many, 22 percent, came from traditional Chinese sources.[6] In his later speeches these references to traditional sources became even more common, while Stalin disappeared. Mao Zedong had become what he had long admired: an emperor of the Legalist school, eager to wield the double-edged sword of totalitarianism and hegemony.[7]

THE LEGALIST RESTORATION

With the establishment of the People's Republic of China on October 1, 1949, both the Chinese people and the world were told that the future had come to China. Viewed from a long-term historical perspective, however, it looked suspiciously like a case of back to the future.[8] To be sure, the ideological rationalization used to justify and legitimate Communist rule differed in many particulars from the statecraft of its Confucian predecessor. The central political myth of Imperial China was that the emperor held his place by divine sanction and led by moral example, and that as long as he maintained Confucian standards of public virtue he would continue to enjoy this "Mandate of Heaven." The central myth of the People's Republic of China, like that of other Communist states, is that the Chinese Communist Party ("the Vanguard of the Proletariat") is temporarily exercising dictatorial power on behalf of the "masses" in anticipation of the early "withering away" of the state.

But if the wineskin was new, its contents remained the bitter gall of vintage Legalism. The CCP takeover reversed the brief efflorescence of civil society in the first decades of the twentieth century, restoring the traditional pattern of state-society relations in which society is almost totally subservient to the state. Veiled in communist terminology and giving formal deference to a theory of civil rights that the emperors would have scorned, Legalism was reborn in China. Communist to all outward appearances, the new Chinese state was Legalist in essence, continuing the autocratic tradition of the imperial Chinese state by

- imposing an official ideology (Marxism-Leninism-Maoism) with interesting functional parallels to Chinese imperial orthodoxy (Legalism-Confucianism);
- concentrating political power in the hands of a tiny minority, often of one, with power deriving ultimately from control of the military and wielded without appreciable institutional constraints;
- treating the penal code and the legal system as tools of governance wielded by the ruler, who acts above legal constraints;

- dominating most, and at times all, aspects of domestic commercial and economic life;
- controlling all forms of social organization outside the nuclear family, while putting severe restrictions upon the latter;
- engaging in political practices familiar from dynastic times, such as large-scale literary persecutions, purges of the bureaucracy, court intrigues, and elite factional conflicts;
- regarding the people as its property, as subjects rather than citizens.

The nascent civil society which had grown up during the Republican era was eradicated as a result of the "reeducation" or execution of those formerly in leadership positions and the destruction or absorption of the organizations they had headed. Newspapers and magazines were brought under state control or closed down entirely. Private and Christian schools were taken over by the state. Voluntary associations were disbanded or amalgamated into Party-led front groups. By the end of the five-year period following 1949, few vestiges of China's once-flourishing civil society still survived. Chinese society had come to resemble that of an archetypal communist state—or equally, that of a Chinese imperial dynasty.[9]

As an emperor of the Legalist school, Mao believed that the Mandate of Heaven gave him license to dominate not only the Chinese people, but all of China's traditional dominions. China's greatness demanded that lost territories be recaptured, straying vassals be recovered, and one-time tributary states be once again forced to follow Beijing's lead. For these reasons Mao intervened in Korea in the early years of his rule, invaded Tibet, bombarded Quemoy, continued to bluster over Taiwan, attacked India over Tibetan border questions, confronted the Soviet Union, and gave massive amounts of military aid to Vietnam.

Maps were drawn up showing China's borders extending far to the north, south and west of the area that the PLA actually controlled. Fr. Seamus O'Reilly, a Columban missionary who was one of the last foreign Catholic priests to leave China in 1953, recalls seeing, in the office of the local communist officials who interrogated him, a map of the PRC that included all of Southeast Asia *within* China's borders.[10]

But such maps were marked for internal distribution only. For Mao, although willing to go to war to restore China's imperium piecemeal, was uncharacteristically coy about his overall imperial aims. Even as his troops were engaged in Korea or Tibet he continually sought to reassure the world, in the policy equivalent of a Freudian slip, "We will never seek hegemony." Once he had vanquished his enemies, Mao may have been open about his dictatorial aims at home, but along his borders he still faced an array of powerful forces. The United States occupied Japan and South Korea, and had bases in the Philippines and Thailand. The British were in Hong Kong and Malaysia. Even his erstwhile ally, the Soviet Union, was occupying large swaths of Chinese territory in Manchuria, Inner Mongolia, and Xinjiang.

"When hemmed in, resort to stratagems," advised Sun-tzu. The diplomatic establishment of the PRC, headed by the charming and crafty Premier Zhou Enlai, developed not just one stratagem, but three. The first was for China to play the role of a loyal member of the Soviet-dominated communist bloc. The second was taking an anti-colonial posture as a member—indeed the leading member—of the Third World, a posture used to great effect with India, for example. The third stratagem, which proved increasingly useful as time went on, was posing as a responsible member of the post-Westphalian international system, a respecter of international agreements and international borders, merely one nation-state among many. As befits a well-designed stratagem, each of these postures seemed to reflect a certain truth about the PRC.

Mao's adopted ideology demanded that lip service, at least, be paid to international communist unity, but the relationship of China's "revolutionary, statesman, theoretician and scientist" with Stalin was complicated from the beginning. Mao was grateful for Stalin's aid, but suspicious that the Soviet leader was trying to keep China disunited and weak, and more often than not rejected his advice. In 1936 he ousted the "28 Bolsheviks" that Stalin's Comintern had foisted upon the CCP, thus reducing Moscow's influence over his guerilla movement. In 1945 he rejected out of hand Stalin's staggering suggestion that he disband his army and join Chiang Kai-shek's government, advice which he later ridiculed.[11]

The USSR's late entry into the war against Japan had allowed Soviet troops to occupy parts of Inner Mongolia, Manchuria, and Xinjiang. Mao could do little about this insult to China's sovereignty until the CCP had emerged victorious in the civil war, when he journeyed to the Soviet Union for two months of hard negotiations with Stalin. The terms of the Treaty of Friendship, Alliance and Mutual Assistance, which Mao and Stalin signed on February 12, 1950, gave Moscow a degree of economic and political leverage within China all too reminiscent of the old colonial days.

By 1958 Mao was publicly expressing unhappiness over the way these negotiations had gone: "In 1950 I argued with Stalin in Moscow for two months. On the questions of the Treaty of Mutual Assistance, the Chinese Eastern Railway, the joint-stock companies and the border we adopted two attitudes: one was to argue when the other side made proposals we did not agree with, and the other was to accept their proposal if they absolutely insisted. This was out of consideration for the interests of socialism."[12]

Despite his unhappiness at Russian "colonialism," Mao had accomplished his principal goals, which were the removal of all Soviet forces from Chinese soil, the return of the China Eastern Railway and Dalian (Port Arthur), and the avoidance of any additional territorial concessions. Mao's determination to recover China's lost grandeur did not include kowtowing to one of the imperialistic powers that had humiliated it, even if it happened to be a member of the same ideological camp. For the Chinese, Soviet ascendance meant domination by a people that, rightly or wrongly, they regarded as culturally inferior. "The hungry land," as they called Russia, was not going to devour any additional Chinese territory.[13]

On January 12, 1950, Secretary of State Dean Acheson gave a speech at the National Press Club, the main thrust of which was that China, left alone by the West, would soon break with the Soviet Union. The Soviet "absorption" of Outer and Inner Mongolia, Xinjiang and Manchuria, he vigorously asserted, was "the most important fact in the relations of any foreign power with Asia." America must avoid conflict with China so as not to "deflect from the Russians to ourself the righteous anger and the wrath and the hatred of the Chinese people which must develop."[14]

Ironically, Acheson's speech is not remembered for its prescience on the issue of a Sino-Soviet split, but for its contribution to the outbreak of hostilities on the Korean Peninsula. Having been assured that Stalin had not targeted South Korea for aggression, Acheson famously failed to include it within the U.S. defense perimeter in Asia, as he defined it. North Korean Communist dictator Kim Il-sung soon thereafter won Stalin's agreement to a limited offensive and, on June 25 of that same year, the entire North Korean army poured across the border and fell upon the almost defenseless south.

This was Mao's first opportunity to reassert China's traditional prerogatives over one-time vassal states. With the world's attention fixed on the Korean Peninsula, he sent elements of the People's Liberation Army to take control of Tibet. The Dalai Lama was forced to sign an agreement on October 21, 1950, acknowledging Chinese sovereignty. Tibet became a protectorate of China, although it would continue, for a time, to control its own domestic affairs.

On the Korean Peninsula the war had quickly turned against Kim Il-sung. By late November 1950, American forces under the command of General Douglas MacArthur were approaching the Yalu River, which separates Korea from China. With his half kingdom fast disappearing, Kim appealed to China for succor—exactly what tributary states were expected to do when threatened by outside powers.

Mao responded promptly with a grand imperial gesture, throwing a huge "volunteer" army into the fray. He was not reacting to a threat but seizing an opportunity, in this case to reestablish Chinese suzerainty over a once and future tributary state.[15] Recklessly inviting casualties, the Chinese army advanced by overwhelming the beleaguered Americans in wave after wave of attacks, eventually forcing them back to a tiny enclave centered around the southern port city of Pusan. A surprise amphibious landing at Inchon turned the tide, cutting the Chinese lines in half. After intense fighting, the front was consolidated near the 38th parallel in October 1951, and Kim Il-sung's half kingdom was restored.

Mao later summed up the Korean War in a 1958 speech to his generals as "a big war in which we defeated America and obtained valuable experience."[16] Viewing Korea strictly as a military contest, Mao's comment may seem mere conceit. After all, the PLA lost at least a quarter of a million men (as opposed to some 34,000 American casualties), gained no territory over the original North-South partition, and settled for a negotiated armistice. Viewed as a bid to recover a tributary state, however, Mao's intervention was an impressive first step. He fought the U.S. to a standstill, establishing China as a military power to be reckoned with. He impressed the Soviets, who had been unwilling to commit ground forces into the fray. Even more importantly, he had brought at least the northern half of the Korean Peninsula back into its traditional relationship of dependency on China. The first step towards the restoration of Chinese hegemony over Asia had been taken.

THE SINO-SOVIET SPLIT

Although Mao was never comfortable with the Soviet domination of the Sino-Soviet relationship, he was for many years careful to avoid open criticism. But Khrushchev's "secret speech" discrediting Stalin, delivered to the CPSU Twentieth Congress in February 1956, marked a turning point. Whatever compunctions Mao may have felt about privately criticizing the Soviet leadership vanished. Talking to the Politburo in 1956, Mao warned, "We must not blindly follow the Soviet Union. . . . Every fart has some kind of smell, and we cannot say that all Soviet farts smell sweet." He was irritated that his countrymen worshipped all things Soviet. He complained at one point he "couldn't have eggs or chicken soup for three years because an article appeared in the Soviet Union which said that one shouldn't eat them. . . . It didn't matter whether the article was current or not, the Chinese listened all the same and respectfully obeyed." He mocked Chinese artists who, when painting pictures of him and Stalin, "always made me a little bit shorter, thus blindly knuckling under to the moral pressure exerted by the Soviet Union at that time."[17] He remained conciliatory in public, however, largely because he was hoping to get his hands on Soviet nuclear weapons.

Mao's eagerness to acquire nuclear weapons, so as to confirm China's newly achieved great power status, knew no bounds. Although he had earlier rejected, as an affront to Chinese sovereignty, a Soviet offer to set up its own nuclear bases on Chinese soil, he somehow managed to convince Stalin's successor to aid China's nuclear weapons program. A nuclear technology transfer agreement to this end was signed in 1957. Under this agreement, Khrushchev later recalled, the Chinese received "almost everything they asked for. We kept no secrets from them. Our nuclear experts co-operated with their engineers and designers who were busy building a bomb."[18]

The Soviets were about to hand over a prototype bomb when Mao's saber rattling over Taiwan spooked them. As Mao prepared to invade Quemoy and Mazu in September 1958, Khrushchev advised caution. Mao was deeply offended, in part because he no longer respected Soviet military advice.[19] So it was that when Khrushchev pointedly reminded him that America possessed nuclear weapons, Mao airily dismissed the possibility of mass casualties. "So what if we lose 300 million people," the Great Helmsman told a stunned Khrushchev. "Our women will make it up in a generation."

Not surprisingly, in June 1959 Khrushchev unilaterally abrogated the agreement that was to have provided China with an atomic weapon.[20] Mao was furious. In September of that year he angrily denounced Soviet meddling in Chinese affairs, telling members of the Military Affairs Commission, "It is absolutely impermissible to go behind the back of our fatherland to collude with a foreign country."[21] The Soviets were "revisionists," China was soon telling the world, and a greater threat than American "imperialism." In going its own way, China was now less a part of an international revolutionary movement than the reawakening Hegemon slowly regaining control over its known world.[22]

With the onset of the Cultural Revolution, the war of words escalated, and armed clashes broke out at several points along the 4,000-mile border with the Soviet Union. Mao dispatched additional troops to the border and on March 2, 1969, on the Chairman's orders, a battalion-sized PLA force ambushed Soviet patrols on the Wusuli River. The Soviets promptly retaliated, and during the next two years there were repeated skirmishes at many points along the border. Though no territory changed hands, the message was clear: The existing border was dependent on Soviet strength, not Chinese acquiescence.

The Ninth Party Congress, held April 1–24 that same year, took an openly hegemonic tone. The only published speech was that of Lin Biao, then Chairman Mao's heir apparent, who repeated Mao's formula that a third world war would promote revolution and dig the graves of both revisionism and imperialism. "We must be ready for a conventional war and also for an atomic war," Lin said. "Both the Soviet Union and the United States are paper tigers." The present border between the Soviet Union and China could be made the basis of negotiation, he avowed, but Moscow would first have to admit that the historical border treaties were "unequal treaties."[23]

STRANGLING TIBET

After PLA troops entered Tibet in 1950, the government of the Dalai Lama was gradually isolated. Those members of the international community who questioned Chinese actions were haughtily informed that the Tibetan question was a purely internal affair. The Himalayan plateau had been an integral part of China for centuries, Beijing's story went, having been brought under China's sway as early as the seventh century, when the Tang Emperor Li Shimin sent his daughter Princess Wencheng as a bride to the great Tibetan king Songtsen Gampo. The princess then bestowed culture on the uncouth Tibetans, bringing them and their land forever into the debt and the orbit of China's superior civilization.

In fact, the emperor sent his favorite daughter, famed for her beauty and talents, as a peace offering to Songsten Gampo because he had a healthy respect for the military prowess of his Himalayan neighbors, not because he intended to civilize them. Had the Tibetan king been seeking a closer association with Chinese culture, the tribute would have flowed the other way.

The Chinese Communists, having promised to respect Tibet's autonomy, instead gradually suffocated its political and religious institutions during the 1950s. Half the land of traditional Tibet was carved up and handed over to other provinces where Chinese were in the majority. The process of Sinicization was accelerated during the chaotic days of the Great Leap Forward, when Mao's cadres carried class warfare into the Land of the Snows, sacking monasteries and killing monks. When the Tibetans rose in protest in 1959, Beijing, claiming that the Tibetan Local Government had "instigated a rebellion," used brute force to consolidate total control.[24]

On March 25, 1959, after heavy fighting, Chinese Communist troops occupied Lhasa. The Dalai Lama fled the capital. Beijing announced that its army had "swiftly put down the rebellion in Lhasa and was mopping up the rebels in some other places in Tibet." The Tibetan government under the Dalai Lama was formally dissolved, replaced by a puppet regime headed by the 21-year-old Panchen Lama. For the first time since the thirteenth century, the Tibetans did not control their own country.[25]

To justify their intervention, the Chinese Communists invented a mythological Tibet where the masses were enslaved by a slothful priestly class. The propaganda machine churned out horror stories of a dark and brutal theocracy of bonded labor, vast monastic fiefs, indolent monks and immoral abbots. As late as 1998 the Chinese Communist Party, in the person of Party Secretary Jiang Zemin, was still patting itself on the back for ending monkish "slavery" in Tibet.[26]

In order to bring the partly nomadic Tibetan population under control, the Chinese herded them into the commune system, a new form of serfdom far worse than anything in Tibet's past. As in China proper, the commune system proved to be an economic and ecological disaster of the first magnitude. Chinese agricultural officials ordered the Tibetans to raise wheat rather than the barley they preferred, and the resulting crop failures on the high Himalayan plain with its short growing season left them malnourished.

Meanwhile, the monasteries and nunneries were emptied and the resident monks and nuns put to work in the communes. The 70,000-character Petition of the Panchen Lama, written in 1962, states that 97 percent of Tibet's 2,000 monasteries were destroyed following the 1959 uprising, presumably by the People's Liberation Army. A few years later, the Cultural Revolution completed this destructive work. All of China suffered from the depredations of Chairman Mao's Red Guards, but Tibet, outside the Chinese cultural sphere, was a special target. Thanks to Beijing's propaganda, these young zealots viewed Tibet as the very embodiment of a corrupt and exploitative feudal tradition, and they set about with picks, shovels, and even their bare hands destroying every religious edifice and artifact they could find. By the time their rampage ended, Tibet's few remaining stupas and lamaseries were in ruins.

WAR WITH INDIA

Nehru insisted on recognizing China's "rights" in Tibet despite the pleas of the Tibetans, along with many Indians, that he weigh in against this new form of Chinese hegemony. His appeasement of the "New China" came back to haunt him in 1959 when the Chinese, having disposed of the Dalai Lama and his followers, began building military roads right up to the existing Indian-Tibetan border, and then, in early September, crossed over into India.

China's aggression took Nehru completely by surprise, which is perhaps less a consequence of his naiveté than of Zhou Enlai's sophisticated sales pitch about the two countries being fellow victims of the Western imperial powers. The Chinese Premier had first visited him in New Delhi in April 1954, stopping over on his way back to China after signing the Geneva peace accord on Indochina. Zhou played the second international stratagem to the hilt, portraying the PRC as a country with impeccable anti-colonialist, anti-imperialist credentials, a country that was a natural member of the Third World club. Nehru agreed.

To be sure, Nehru had been favorably disposed toward the People's Republic of China from the beginning. India had been the first "capitalist" country to recognize China (in April 1950), the leading non-communist proponent for admitting the PRC into the U.N., and the principal intermediary between Beijing and Washington during the Korean War.

The result of Zhou's 1954 visit was a joint communiqué based on China's "Five Principles of Peaceful Coexistence." Nehru breathlessly announced that relations between India and China would henceforth be governed by "mutual respect for territorial sovereignty, mutual non-aggression, mutual non-intervention in internal affairs, equality and mutual benefit, and peaceful coexistence." These high-sounding principles were reaffirmed at the April 1955 Conference of Asian Countries in New Delhi, and again at the Conference of Asian and African Countries in Bandung, Indonesia.[27] By now, Nehru had assumed the role of Zhou's patron, eager to advance Zhou's cause by smoothing over China's past support for destabilizing guerilla movements throughout the region. For his part Zhou spoke of the "Bandung Spirit," a new policy of peacefully wooing nonaligned nations in the region according to the Five Principles. Mesmerized by the Five Principles and the Bandung Spirit, Nehru could not bring himself to see that India and China had fundamentally divergent interests.

The Indian delegation at the U.N. was arguing passionately on behalf of Communist China's admission to the General Assembly on the very day that PLA troops began pouring across the border into India. As Nehru pondered Chinese perfidy, PLA troops continued their march southward, seizing two important mountain passes that guard approaches to Sikkim and India.[28]

Nehru allowed two years of border skirmishes before responding to the pleas of his generals for leave to stop the slow-moving Chinese steamroller. Then the ill-planned Indian attack proved a disaster, and the Chinese advance picked up speed. As tens of thousands of square miles of disputed territory passed into Chinese control, Nehru panicked and requested help from the Soviet Union and America. Moscow blasted the Chinese advance, and the Seventh

Fleet steamed up the Bay of Bengal. The Chinese, having gotten what they wanted, offered a cease-fire. An overwrought Nehru, who had begun to have nightmares about Chinese troops on the Ganges, was only too glad to accept.

EXPANSION BY GUERRILLA

The PRC had initially supported Maoist-style Communist parties in Malaysia, Indonesia, Japan, Burma, India and Thailand. The Malaysian Communist Party launched an armed rebellion, which the PRC supported until it became clear that the guerrillas were losing. At the Bandung conference, a conciliatory Zhou Enlai declared that those Chinese who adopted another nationality should be good citizens of the countries they joined. But this pious statement did not completely allay suspicions that China was encouraging indigenous communist movements among the "bridge compatriots" of Southeast Asia.

After the invasion of India, Beijing once more began manifesting a new militancy toward countries in Southeast Asia. The Bandung Spirit was a thing of the past. Instead, Communist China began to act in accordance with an ancient Chinese diplomatic principle, *yuan chiao chin kung,* meaning "to appease distant countries while attacking those nearby."[29] Faraway Canada, Italy, Belgium, Chile, and Mexico were courted for diplomatic recognition, while neighboring countries like Burma, Indonesia, Thailand, India, and Laos were attacked in word, and sometimes, in deed.

Laos, one of three Indo-China States covered by SEATO protection, was a specific target. Although small in size and population, the country was important because of its strategic location between China, North Vietnam, and the non-communist states of Burma, Thailand, Cambodia, and South Vietnam. A communist guerrilla group, the Pathet Lao, began receiving increasing amounts of military aid in the late fifties. The U.S. countered with an expanding program of military and economic assistance. The conflict intensified in 1959 as North Vietnam sent military units across the border to reinforce the Pathet Lao. On September 4, Laos appealed to the United Nations to dispatch an emergency force to counter aggression by North Vietnam. The U.S. responded by warning both the Soviet Union and Communist China that it would help counter any new danger to peace in the region. China responded by stepping up its aid to the Pathet Lao.

In Indonesia as well, the local Communist Party, responding in part to encouragement and aid from Beijing, launched a coup against General Sukarno's increasingly restive generals in 1962. This particular gambit backfired on Beijing. The result was a bloody purge of suspected Communists which quickly developed anti-Chinese overtones. As many as a million lives were lost, many of them Chinese. The food distribution system and other large sectors of the economy, which had been run by this mercantile minority, consequently collapsed.

TAIWAN

It was the recovery of Taiwan that remained Mao's principal obsession. No sooner was the Korean armistice in place than the Great Helmsman ordered the PLA to begin preparing for the invasion of Taiwan that would mark the delayed final battle of the Chinese civil war. There was only one problem: the PLA invading force would have to cross the 90-mile-wide Taiwan Strait, which was patrolled by the carriers and cruisers of the U.S. Seventh Fleet. Moreover, the Nationalist Army was growing more formidable, as a U.S. Military Assistance Advisory Group helped to train and equip its expanding ranks.

China's state-owned press, on August 14, 1954, issued a blistering denunciation of the "American imperialists" for their continued "occupation of Taiwan." The island would be "liberated," by force if necessary.[30] Battle-hardened Communist divisions were moved to staging areas along the Fujian Coast and MiGs appeared over the South China Sea.

Chiang Kai-shek did not back down. He put the Nationalist Army on alert and strengthened his garrisons on the offshore island groups his forces still controlled. Neither did the PRC's bellicosity unnerve President Eisenhower. When the question of Communist China's war preparations came up at a press conference on August 17, he replied that he had recently reaffirmed standing orders to the U.S. Seventh Fleet to defend Taiwan against any attack. "Any invasion of Formosa," the former general remarked, referring to the island by its Portuguese name, "would have to run over the Seventh Fleet."[31]

Deterred from launching a full-scale attack on Taiwan, the Communists shifted their attention to the offshore islands. Chief among these were the Dazhens, located midway between Shanghai and Keelung; the Mazus, ten miles off the port of Fuzhou and opposite the northern end of Taiwan; and the Jinmens (Quemoys), two miles off the port of Xiamen (Amoy). These islands had helped the Republic of China and the U.S. to maintain a fairly effective blockade of the South China coast, and had also served as intelligence gathering posts and commando bases. Both Chiang and Mao regarded these islands as stepping stones. Mao was as eager to capture the offshore islands preparatory to an invasion of Taiwan as Chiang was to employ them as staging areas in the eventual recapture of the mainland.[32]

On September 3 the Chinese Communists began an intense artillery bombardment of Jinmen and Little Jinmen. The Nationalist Air Force responded by bombing Communist artillery positions on the mainland. Fearing that an invasion was imminent, the Nationalist government requested U.S. aid. Eisenhower, however, preferred to wait until an actual assault materialized and it could be seen whether the landing was limited in scope or preliminary to one on Taiwan. His position—defend Taiwan but not the offshore islands—was shortly to be written into the Mutual Defense Treaty of December 2, 1954.[33]

Taking Eisenhower's wait-and-see attitude as a signal that the Americans would not intervene, the Chinese Communists assaulted the northernmost island in the Dazhen chain, a place called I-Jiang Shan, on January 20, 1955. The garrison force of 720 soldiers died to the last man defending the tiny island. Convinced that the two remaining Dazhen Islands were indefensible, Eisenhower pressured Chiang Kai-shek to abandon the chain, offering the U.S. Seventh Fleet to cover the evacuation of the 20,000 civilians and

11,000 Nationalist soldiers stationed there. Chiang reluctantly gave way, withdrawing the last of his forces on February 6, 1955.

At the same time, Eisenhower warned the Chinese Communists that the U.S. would resist an attack on the remaining offshore islands, with nuclear weapons if necessary. To further clarify the American position, Eisenhower asked Congress on January 25 to pass a resolution authorizing him "to assure the security of Formosa and the Pescadores" and, if need be, other "closely related localities" which he did not identify. This resolution, which passed on February 26, convincingly demonstrated to Beijing that the American President and Congress were united in their intention to resist further attacks on Nationalist-held territory. It emphatically underlined the importance of the Sino-American Mutual Defense Treaty, which had been ratified by the Senate just a few weeks before. Not only was Taiwan an indispensable link in the chain of U.S. mutual security agreements ringing Communist China, but the defensive perimeter of the Treaty itself was in effect extended to the offshore islands.[34]

The use of force had given the Communists nothing except an insignificant chain of islands. Faced with a virtual promise of heavy U.S. retaliation in the event of any further attacks, Mao shifted course. The shelling of Jinmen and Mazu came to an abrupt halt, as did the feverish preparations for an assault on the islands. The ever-genial Zhou Enlai arrived at the Bandung conference, held in Indonesia in April 1955, bearing an olive branch: the PRC was willing to sit down with the U.S. at the negotiating table to discuss ways to ease cross-Strait tension.[35]

By the end of May, an informal cease-fire held on the Taiwan Strait. Talks between the U.S. and the PRC began in Geneva and dragged on for months. Washington repeatedly pressed for a joint renunciation of the use of force in the Taiwan area. Beijing balked at this, favoring instead a toothless pronouncement on world peace, and only in exchange for ministerial-level talks. Seventy-three sessions were held in all, but the impasse went on. No formal armistice was ever reached, nor did Beijing agree—then or ever—to renounce the use of force.[36]

Instead, the Chinese Communists continued building up their military establishment opposite Taiwan, and constructed a number of new airfields. In the face of this militancy, the U.S. in 1957 deployed Matador surface-to-surface missiles, capable of carrying nuclear weapons, to Taiwan. Construction began on a major air base near Taichung, in central Taiwan, with a runway long enough to accommodate B-52 strategic bombers. For its part, the ROC fortified the offshore islands and reinforced the garrisons stationed there.

When the Soviet Union in 1957 launched *Sputnik*, the first space satellite, Mao saw it as proof that the Communist bloc had surged ahead of the United States, and he was eager to press its newly won strategic advantage. Following a meeting with Nikita Khrushchev in Beijing, he suddenly unleashed a fierce bombardment on Jinmen on August 23, 1958. Tens of thousands of artillery rounds rained down on the island while Communist jets launched strafing attacks. Offshore, torpedo boats attacked Nationalist convoy and transport ships. On August 29, Radio Beijing announced that an amphibious landing on Jinmen was imminent. The 100,000-man Nationalist garrison on the island was on alert as PRC torpedo boats continued swarming about the island and gunners concentrated their fire on Jinmen's landing beach and airstrip, rendering them unusable. But the threat of invasion had been a feint: the real intent had been to impose a blockade. It was only a matter of time before the garrison force, deprived of reinforcements and supplies from Taiwan, would be starved out.

Eisenhower, realizing that the PRC's ultimate objective remained the capture of Taiwan itself, publicly warned the regime not to attempt an invasion of the offshore islands. "Let us suppose that the Chinese Communists conquer Quemoy," he remarked in a radio address. "Would that be the end of the story? . . . They frankly say that their present military effort is part of a program to conquer Formosa. . . . [T]his plan would liquidate all of the free world positions in the Western Pacific."[37] To demonstrate its commitment to the defense of Taiwan, the U.S. immediately shipped a host of modern weapons to the island. To emphasize the point, Nationalist Chinese and American Marines, on September 8, staged a large-scale amphibious landing on southern Taiwan.

Meanwhile, the blockade of Jinmen had continued for two weeks, until on September 7 a convoy of Nationalist supply ships, escorted by warships of the U.S. Seventh Fleet and the ROC Navy, steamed directly for the beleaguered island. The U.S. naval squadron escorted the supply ships to a point three nautical miles from Jinmen, then stood off while they continued on to land and unload their cargo. The commander of the U.S. squadron had permission to return fire if fired upon, but the Communist guns were silent. Mao had blinked.[38]

Still, Beijing's bizarre behavior persisted. An "even-day" cease-fire was announced on October 25 and gradually became a regular part of island life. On even days, convoys could arrive without being challenged; on odd days, the attack continued, but with diminishing intensity. The Taiwan press condemned this as a cruel game. Eisenhower called it a Gilbert and Sullivan war.

Eventually the Taiwan Strait crisis passed. The Eisenhower-Dulles policy of facing down Communist aggression wherever it might occur, along with the resolve of the Nationalist government, had prevailed. At the same time, the failure of the Great Leap Forward and the ensuing famine, along with unrest in Tibet, may have turned the attention of the Communists to their growing domestic problems for a while.[39] Although the artillery bombardments would continue sporadically for decades afterwards, the Chinese Communists would never again challenge the Nationalist government over the offshore islands.[40]

BLOODY BORDERS

Because of its peace-loving rhetoric, the People's Republic of China has largely avoided the reputation for bellicosity that its history deserves. In the few short decades of its existence, PRC has intervened in Korea, assaulted and absorbed Tibet, supported guerilla movements throughout Southeast Asia, attacked India, fomented an insurrection in Indonesia, provoked border clashes with the Soviet Union, and instigated repeated crises vis-à-vis Taiwan.

When an opportunity arose to send out China's legions, Mao and his successors generally did not hesitate—especially if the crises involved a former tributary state, which is to say almost all of the countries with which China has a common border. Although the PRC is not as well known for its militarism as the Islamic states, it has far more often resorted to violence in settling international disputes. Up to 1987, China had employed violence in fully 76.9 percent of its international crises. The comparable figure for the Muslim states was 53.5 percent. China's propensity for violence is even more striking when compared to the Soviet Union (28.5 percent), the United States (17.9 percent), and the United Kingdom (11.5 percent). China, to paraphrase the scholar Samuel Huntington, has bloody borders.[41]

CHAPTER FOUR

Great Han Chauvinism

O n his own terms, Mao Zedong was a failure. Eager to restore China's lost grandeur, recover its still-alienated territories, and once again dominate the vast marches of Asia, the founder of the People's Republic of China cannot be said to have succeeded on any front. His failures were spectacular, to be sure, but they were failures nonetheless. The socialization of industry, the collectivization of agriculture, the Great Leap Forward, and the Cultural Revolution, to name just a few of his incessant political campaigns, failed to lift China into the first rank of nations.

More to the point, Mao died without achieving his goal of reunifying all of Greater China. The same Marxist-Leninist ideology which propelled him to victory in the Chinese civil war paradoxically denied him the economic clout and military means necessary to rebuild the Chinese imperium. He recovered Manchuria from the Japanese, Inner Mongolia and Xinjiang from the Soviets, Tibet from the Tibetans, and half of Korea from the Americans, but beyond this his hegemonic ambitions were frustrated. Large parts of Greater China, including Taiwan, the South China Sea, Mongolia, the Russian Far East and Central Asia, remained outside of his control. As Mao complained to Henry Kissinger in 1973, "[I]n history the Soviet Union has carved out one and a half million square kilometers from China."[1]

Unlike earlier emperors, Mao's writ ended at his borders. The rest of Asia was dominated by two powers: the "socialist imperialist" Soviet Union, which held sway over the landmass to the north and west, and the "capitalist imperialist" United States and its allies, which ruled the oceans and territories to the east and south.

At the time of Mao's death in 1976, China had unresolved irredentist claims in every direction of the compass: to the north and west in the Soviet Union, to the south in South and Southeast Asia, and to the east in Taiwan, the Philippines and Japan. Yet Mao's failure to act on these claims reflected a lack of means, not a lack of will. If China had possessed a blue water navy and a modern air force in the fifties, Mao would have tried to take Taiwan by force. If China had enjoyed the same advantage over the Soviet Union that, say, the U.S. enjoys over Canada, there is no doubt that Mao would have abrogated the 1860 Sino-Russian Treaty of Beijing, in which the Qing government ceded the territory that is now the Russian Far East.

Mao's primal mistake, if it could be called that, was in choosing as the instrument of China's national aggrandizement an economic policy totally inadequate to the task of rebuilding a Hegemon that could compete with twentieth century capitalism. True, communism was the perfect vehicle for achieving the second half of the essential Legalist program of "enriching the state and strengthening the military," but not the first. Communism enabled Mao to recruit and effectively deploy a huge standing army and police force, and to concentrate all *existing* economic resources in the hands of the state. Communism brought China Proper under his control. But the strength of Maoism, like its imperial predecessor, was in reducing the people to obedience rather than producing an abundance of goods. Communism was simply incapable of generating new wealth and technology at the rate that capitalism did; this made it difficult for a communist nation to equip its army, however vast, with weapons sophisticated enough to challenge its capitalist adversaries.

By the end of his life, Mao was increasingly frustrated by the economic setbacks of his years in power. He chose to blame them on what he called his "lack of training in economics." But China's economic difficulties were not such that enrolling Chairman Mao in a macroeconomics course, save one taught by Milton Friedman, would have helped. And Mao would certainly have had Milton Friedman shot for questioning Legalism's primary presupposition:

that power politics deserves primacy over private economic transactions.

THE "FOUR MODERNIZATIONS"

Only a quarter-century after Mao Zedong's death, it sometimes seems to foreigners that his views have been completely repudiated by the current ruling elite. Nothing could be further from the truth. Mao's rule was mostly good (70 percent) and only partly bad (30 percent), according to today's Party dogma. While it is true that Mao's economics has long since been abandoned in favor of a kind of marketized Marxism, on many other issues China's political elite continues to hold opinions identical to the late chairman's. On the question of China's proper place in the world or the recovery of Taiwan, for instance, there is no daylight between the views of Mao Zedong and his successors, Deng Xiaoping and Jiang Zemin.

Deng Xiaoping did clash seriously with Mao over economic issues. During the fifties, when Mao sought to streamline China's socialist economy by eradicating "selfishness," his principal means were forced collectivization and endless moral exhortations. Deng, on the other hand, accepted self-interest as a fact of life. After the disastrous Great Leap Forward, he and Liu Shaoqi, the head of state, sought to stimulate productivity by offering garden plots to peasants and bonuses to workers. Mao saw these practices as corrupting the "New Socialist Man" he was trying to create. At the beginning of the Great Proletarian Cultural Revolution in 1966, he ordered Deng and Liu arrested.

Deng's fall from grace could easily have been fatal. So it proved to be for Liu Shaoqi, who was tortured to death by his Red Guard captors for continuing to insist on his innocence after Mao had declared his guilt. Deng, on the other hand, readily admitted that he had made mistakes, but maintained that his "intentions" had been correct.[2] By this he meant that he had always been loyal to the Great Helmsman and to his goal of building a New China, modern and strong. He had erred in opposing Maoist means only because he had been so intent on achieving Mao's larger goals. Deng's distinction between means and ends probably saved his life, but it was more than a clever ploy. On the essential Legalist program of "enriching the state and strengthening the military," he and Mao saw eye to eye.

Following his rehabilitation in 1973, Deng played to his strength, developing with then-Premier Zhou Enlai a new campaign to modernize and strengthen China that became known as the "Four Modernizations." Zhou had first broached the idea in a 1964 speech, advocating the "comprehensive modernization of agriculture, industry, national defense, and science and technology by the end of the century." Now in early 1975 he returned to this theme, proposing in his "Report on the Work of the Government" to the National People's Congress that China undertake to modernize in these four key areas.

The Four Modernizations were merely Legalism restated. Modernizing "agriculture" and "industry" enriched the state and modernizing the "national defense" strengthened the military, while modernizing "science and technology" benefited both. As a set of goals, the Four Modernizations were unobjectionable to Chairman Mao and enjoyed the enthusiastic support of the vast majority of the Chinese political elite, who were eager to see China return to Asian preeminence. As the discussion shifted to methods, however, the same old differences between Deng and the Maoist radicals emerged more sharply than ever.

Deng, by now First Vice-Premier, began pushing for material incentives, more academic specialization, and the import of foreign technology. The radicals responded by maligning Deng as the "bourgeois within the communist party," whose policies would lead to a restoration of capitalism in China. When Deng and his allies drafted a series of documents on modernization, industrialization, and the development of science and technology, the radicals stripped him of all his posts in 1976 and once again sent him into internal exile.[3]

But Mao's death later that year led to the arrest of the Maoist radicals, now stigmatized as the Gang of Four. Deng returned in triumph to the capital. The Chinese people, their primitive economy threadbare and their morale exhausted by the disastrous years of the Cultural Revolution, welcomed him with open arms, pleased by the prospect he offered of an end to brutal political campaigns and the promise of a better material life. But the Chinese elite, Deng included, had fundamentally different aspirations. Beijing's phrase-makers called the Four Modernizations program "The New Long March," and looked forward with confidence (and prescience as well) to the year 2000, when China would have arrived at a state of relative modernity and become a military and economic power to be reckoned with.

A Legalist program to strengthen China and allow it to resume regional hegemony carried the day. Under Deng's guiding hand, the egalitarian ethos of Maoism was abandoned in favor of market incentives, while state planning increasingly took a back seat to the organized chaos of the free market. The agricultural communes were abandoned in favor of family farms, and privately owned businesses sprang up all over the country. China opened up to the West, which proved more than willing to enter into joint ventures with Chinese firms, transfer the technology needed to set up new production lines, and buy the cheap goods that resulted.

This greater economic openness was never an end in itself—though it is viewed as such by many foreigners and some Chinese—but merely the means to an end: a wealthy and powerful Chinese state. Deng gambled that temporarily weakening the state by relaxing its stranglehold over the economy would strengthen it over the long run through economic growth—a wager that he arguably won, since the Chinese economy has been expanding at a double-digit clip for most of the past twenty years.

"To get rich is glorious," Deng is well known for saying; he might well have added, *sotto voce*, "To strengthen the state is divine." Though it no longer plans the economy down to the last ounce of steel, the Chinese state effectively controls vastly more resources today than it did in 1979. Deng's Four Modernizations were really the Legalist ends in another guise, while his much-vaunted openness to the West was merely a ploy to enlist foreigners to provide the means. Both were highly successful.

THE "FOUR ABSOLUTES"

"Pragmatic reformer" though he might have been, Deng did not consider it a contradiction to be firmly committed to Chinese autocracy. Alongside his Four Modernizations, he added a fourfold stricture called the Four Absolutes. These were the dictatorship of the proletariat, the leadership of the Communist Party, Marxism-Leninism-Mao Zedong Thought, and the socialist road. Despite the economic reforms on which it had embarked, Deng was saying, the Chinese Communist Party-state would continue to maintain its monopoly on political power, impose an official ideology, and firmly control its subjects, much as China's ancient Legalists had taught.

Deng Xiaoping's commitment to the Four Absolutes was tested on Tiananmen Square some eleven years later. For seven weeks in the spring of 1989, the Chinese people put on a spectacular show of defiance against the regime and its aging leader. By the end of May, a million or more people were surging through the streets of Beijing in protest of corruption, bureaucracy, and dictatorship. Deng's unwavering answer to these peaceful, nonviolent protests was deadly force, even if its use meant, as he put it, "spilling a little blood." On the night of June 4, as the West watched in horror, the People's Liberation Army opened fire on unarmed demonstrators with automatic weapons and ran them down with tanks and armored personnel carriers. By morning the dictatorship of the proletariat was once again firmly in place.

For the Deng-led leadership, the killing of thousands of demonstrators was no accidental mishap. The ruling elite had got exactly what it wanted from the cold-blooded killing: the renewed submission of the Chinese people to its rule and the perpetuation of its monopoly on power. When Secretary of State James A. Baker III told Premier Li Peng that Tiananmen was a "tragedy," Li would have none of it. "The actions in Tiananmen Square were a good thing," he retorted. "We do not regard them as a tragedy."[4]

The paradox of Deng Xiaoping still puzzles many in the West. How could the chief architect of China's market reforms also be the master butcher of Tiananmen? To resolve this riddle they imagine that Deng was afflicted with a kind of schizophrenia that made

him part pragmatic liberal and part orthodox socialist revolutionary. The twists and turns of the reform process, with its alternat-
ing phases of liberal relaxation and conservative retrenchment, they
attribute to Deng's supposed ambivalence as he was driven first
by one set of impulses, then by another.[5]

But Deng did not suffer from the political equivalent of bipo-
lar disorder. It is just that debates over economic policy are conducted with the Communist Party leadership in a fundamentally
different fashion from debates over politics. The economic debate
revolves about the *means* of power; the political debate is over
the *ends* of power. One could be "pragmatic," even "liberal," when
discussing economic policy while remaining "orthodox" and "conservative" when discussing politics. The economic debate is relatively open to participation and tolerant of diverging views; the
political debate is closed to all but the top leaders, and is a dangerous game even for them. Disagreeing with the leadership on, say,
the privatization of state-owned enterprises is not a career-ending
move; an official can always argue, as Deng had with his Red Guard
captors during the Cultural Revolution, that his intentions are
good—i.e., that his proposed policies will "enrich the state and
strengthen the military." Disagreeing with the leadership on when
to enforce the Four Absolutes or to assert Chinese hegemony, however, can be politically fatal. So it was for two of Deng's chosen successors, Hu Yaobang and Zhao Ziyang, both of whom he cashiered
for such political incorrectness before settling upon a third, Jiang
Zemin. Jiang survived in power because he demonstrated a Deng-
like grasp of the threat posed by political reform as opposed to
the economic variety, whereas Zhao, who did not, has spent the
last decade under house arrest.[6]

HEGEMONY UNDER DENG

Deng had joined the Community Party around the same time as
Mao, in the early 1920s, and for the same reasons: Both believed
that this newly founded organization and its governing ideology
could return to China the dignity and unity it had lost to the invading imperialist powers. The short, taciturn general was a study in

contrasts beside the large, voluble Mao; he cared nothing for the trappings of office, wrote no poetry, and had no imperial pretensions, being content to wield authority from his lowly post as Vice Premier. Yet he possessed the same conviction of Chinese superiority over neighboring peoples, near and distant. Only the complete recovery of China's lost possessions and its hegemonic status would fully vindicate China's humiliation at the hands of perceived inferiors.

Hong Kong and Taiwan were at the top of Deng's hit list. He was a bulldog during the 1982 negotiations with Prime Minister Margaret Thatcher over the future of the British Crown Colony of Hong Kong. Thatcher originally insisted on the continuing validity of the treaties under which the Qing dynasty had permanently ceded Kowloon and Hong Kong to the British crown, and sought to renegotiate the lease on the New Territories, set to expire on June 30, 1997. Deng insisted that the British were only in Hong Kong on Chinese sufferance, and that China could and would resume sovereignty over the entire colony whenever it so chose. A further blast came from the New China News Agency, which in a September 30 press release said that "the unequal treaties" were "illegal, and therefore null and void." The Communist Chinese government would not shirk its "sacred mission" to recover Hong Kong, thus righting the wrong done by British imperialism against China a century before.[7]

In the end, it was the Iron Lady who broke. Once she accepted the Chinese position that the British were in Hong Kong illegally, only the details of the transfer of power remained to be negotiated.

Deng, who up to this point had been opaque about the coming Communist Chinese rule in Hong Kong, dropped a series of bombshells on June 22, 1984. Dashing hopes of a "three-legged stool," he declared that Hong Kong would have no separate voice in the negotiations. The interests of the ethnic Chinese residents of Hong Kong would be represented by the Communist Chinese government, not by the British or the people of Hong Kong themselves. Then he revealed that the People's Liberation Army would be stationed in Hong Kong after 1997. When reminded by Hong

Kong reporters of earlier promises that the PLA would be kept out of Hong Kong, he barked "bullshit," and dared them to "now go and print it."[8]

While Deng wanted to assert political control over his prize, he also respected the economic power that Hong Kong would lend to his modernization efforts. To preserve Hong Kong's "capitalist system and lifestyle," he originated the novel idea of "one country, two systems." Hong Kong's successful reunification under this formula, he reasoned, might ultimately also entice Taiwan back into China's grip. Yet he also placed clear limits on Hong Kong's "second system." He reserved to the "Chinese People's Government" the right to appoint Hong Kong's chief executive and senior officials, and he vetoed later efforts (admittedly feeble) by British governors to move in the direction of self-rule. And when, on June 30, 1997, Hong Kong reverted to Chinese rule, the People's Liberation Army did indeed march in.

Deng also accepted the Chinese imperial "burden" of overseeing the "less-cultured" peoples living on China's periphery. This view of neighboring peoples was intensified by reports from the substantial Chinese minorities residing among them. When, for instance, tens of thousands of ethnic Chinese fled Vietnam for their ancestral land in the late seventies, tales of their brutal persecution by the Vietnamese regime circulated widely in China, angering officials and ordinary folk alike. Following Vietnam's invasion of Cambodia, a Chinese ally, in the autumn of 1978, Deng convened a meeting of the Military Affairs Commission to discuss this new insult. He proposed that the pro-Soviet Vietnamese leadership be taught a lesson, and the members of the MAC wholeheartedly concurred. During his post-normalization goodwill visit to the U.S. in late January 1979, Deng telegraphed his intention.

No sooner had Deng returned to Beijing than a Chinese expeditionary force numbering 330,000 men poured across the border. The Chinese, who euphemistically termed their invasion a "self-defensive counterattack," expected to inflict a quick, decisive defeat on the Vietnamese army. Instead, the PLA was bloodied by 150,000 well-armed and battle-tested Vietnamese defenders. By the time

Deng declared victory and moved to withdraw, 26,000 PLA soldiers had been killed and another 37,000 had been wounded.[9]

The Chinese leadership was privately unhappy with the way the campaign had been prosecuted. Vietnam "was only hurt a little" in its war with China, Chen Yun complained. "We didn't break their fingers, but merely hurt them. In some respects, we actually helped them." MAC Vice-Chairman Nie Rongzhen was said to have called the tactics employed against Vietnam "unsatisfactory."[10]

Still, the PRC had reason enough to declare victory. The invading force had driven far enough into Vietnam to capture four county seats. Even more importantly, after the conflict Hanoi seemed to ease its persecution of its Chinese minority; the stream of refugees fleeing northward died down to a trickle. And if Vietnam had not been taught a lesson, China's other neighbors had. Two lessons, actually. The first was that if you seriously mistreated your Chinese minority, the PRC would intervene, perhaps militarily. The second was that if you attacked an ally of China's, there was a good chance that China would attack you in turn.

PLAYING THE AMERICA CARD

Deng knew that China's border clashes with the Soviet Union, combined with a perception that the Soviets were winning the Cold War against the Americans, had led Zhou Enlai to attempt to redress this growing imbalance of power. With Mao's blessing, he threw China's weight to the perceived weaker side, the United States. That China and the U.S. lacked common values and institutions and, in the years before the U.S.-China trade assumed significant dimensions, a common economic interest, did not matter. With Zhou, as Henry Kissinger was later to remark, "Only one principle was inviolate. No nation would be permitted to be preeminent."[11] China was drawn into a condominium with the U.S. solely out of fear of growing Soviet might, a fear which Kissinger, for his part, did everything in his power to exaggerate.

But as the years passed with no further border clashes between Chinese and Soviet troops, Deng became increasingly suspicious of Henry Kissinger's overwrought claims about the Soviet military threat to China, and uncertain about the notion that power was actually shifting in the direction of the USSR. We don't pay much attention to the Soviet threat, he told Kissinger when the latter visited China in November 1974, going on to say that "the Soviet military strength in the East is not just directed against China. It is also directed against Japan and your Seventh Fleet, your air and naval forces." Deng's increasing and bluntly expressed reluctance to regard the Soviets as a clear and present danger so irritated Kissinger that he began privately referring to Deng as "a nasty little man."[12]

Deng also had begun to look askance at U.S. involvement in crises around the world. "The U.S. is always in the forefront," he objected to Kissinger during this same visit, pointing to Cyprus and the Middle East as examples. He went on to draw a parallel between U.S. intervention in these crises "and the Indochina issue and the Korean issue too." Kissinger attempted to bring the conversation back to the Soviet threat, suggesting to Deng that in "firing cannons [at the U.S.]" he "should not hit [his] own fortifications." "They haven't," Deng replied tersely, in effect dismissing any suggestion of a common defense against the USSR.[13]

The following autumn when Kissinger was next in China, Deng went even further. "We have always believed that we should rely on our independent strength to deal with the Soviet Union," he told Kissinger. ". . . China fears nothing under heaven or on earth. China will not ask favors from anyone. . . . We rely on millet plus rifles to deal with all problems internationally and locally, including the problems in the East [with the Soviet Union]."[14]

An irritated Kissinger reported to President Ford that U.S.-China relations had taken a turn for the worse because of the Chinese leadership's "insolent behavior and self-righteous lack of responsiveness."[15] But Kissinger's expectation of a Sino-American entente, which had led him to make preemptive concessions on Taiwan and other issues, was overblown from the beginning.[16] It seems unlikely that Deng and the Chinese leadership, mindful of past conflicts with America and anticipating a future of Chinese hegemony, had ever intended anything more than a temporary accommodation. Deng's

Four Modernizations policy, with its voracious appetite for foreign trade, technology and capital, began in the late seventies to generate common economic interests, but did not move the two countries any further towards political compatibility.

In fact, just the opposite seemed to occur. By the 1980s, increasingly confident in China's growing economic strength, Deng was truculently informing every foreign visitor he saw, whether from communist or capitalist countries, that no one was entitled to tell China what to do.[17] Without specifying, he left no doubt that he was talking about the U.S.

As the military buildup under President Reagan eclipsed the might of the former Soviet Union, Deng began actively working to improve relations between China and the USSR. It was largely on Deng's initiative that Gorbachev visited Beijing in May 1989. When the Soviet Union collapsed and America emerged triumphant as the sole superpower, Deng further altered his course in opposition. No nation will be permitted to be preeminent, one can almost hear China's Paramount Leader saying, unless of course that nation is China.[18]

THE CURRENT LEADERSHIP

The man who made the decision to "spill a little blood" in Tiananmen in 1989 is now dead, along with most of the party elders who backed him at the time. All of the current members of the Politburo Standing Committee, the Chinese Communist Party's top body, assumed office after Tiananmen with the exception of Li Peng, then premier and now chairman of the National People's Congress. The economic reforms initiated under Deng have produced striking advances, and an ever larger sector of the economy operates outside of state control. Internet use is growing rapidly, Marxist-Leninist-Maoist thought is moribund, and there is little talk of the Four Absolutes in the state-controlled press.

Yet, to a degree unequalled by any other nation in the world, the more China changes, the more it remains the same. Under Jiang Zemin the Middle Kingdom is still an autocratic state, in some respects more so than it was at the time of Tiananmen. The crackdown on political dissent that Chairman Jiang ordered prior to President Clinton's 1998 visit to China did not end with his departure, but intensified throughout 1999. Jiang's justification for the continuing crackdown, articulated in a December 1998 speech, was the need to maintain "social stability," a frequently used euphemism for the government's iron-fisted control of society. Sounding a lot like Mao, Jiang said, "Whenever any element that undermines stability raises its head, it must be resolutely cut off."

Jiang's commitment to reanimating the Hegemon can be seen in his policy initiatives: bracketing Taiwan with missiles, constructing a military base on Mischief Reef in the South China Sea, announcing that the PLA Navy intends to dominate the sea lanes out to the "first island chain," altering the PLA Air Force's defensive posture to one of attack readiness, and deploying a new nuclear-capable missile, the DF-31, able to reach the western United States.[19]

Given such strong actions, why would fifty recently retired PLA generals sign a "strong protest" against President Jiang Zemin's "weak" policies toward the U.S., Japan, and Taiwan, as was reported in Hong Kong in early 1999? Whatever else such a protest signifies, what it does *not* mean is that Jiang is a "closet democrat," a "liberal reformer," or even a "moderate." (The generals are "conservatives," the fuzzy logic goes, and therefore the target of their protest must be a "liberal.") Nor does it mean that the leadership is at odds'over fundamental questions such as China's long-term strategic goals. Jiang and his generals (most of whom he promoted to command rank in the first place) are of one mind that Taiwan should be recovered, Japan neutralized, and the U.S. driven from Asia. But the generals are impatient to act now, while Jiang wants to wait until China is stronger.[20]

Premier Zhu Rongji, Jiang's second-in-command, is another Chinese leader widely regarded in the West as a "moderate." Responsible for China's economy, Zhu has pushed for further economic reforms, for China's membership in the World Trade Organization, and for downsizing inefficient state-owned enterprises. Yet there is no reason to think that, on political or international issues, Zhu is any less of a hardliner than Jiang—or the hardline PLA generals, for that matter. When Zhu receives standing ovations from military audiences, as he reportedly does, it is for emphasizing China's growing strength, not for advocating closer ties to the U.S.

The notion that China's economic reformers harbor a secret admiration for the open society is a Western conceit. U.S.-style democracy has *no* advocates within the senior ranks of the government. The Chinese political elite understand the current openness to the West as an effort to enlist foreigners to provide the means for the restoration of China's greatness. The legacy of Legalism continues to govern Beijing's view of the world today. Jiang Zemin and other leaders are all followers of this aspect of Deng Xiaoping Thought, which is not all that different from Mao Zedong Thought.

Because of Deng's reforms, continued under Jiang and Zhu, China has transformed itself over the past 25 years from an isolated, largely agrarian state to a growing economic and military power. Were he alive today, Chairman Mao would not be pleased by the end of egalitarian economics, but he would be greatly mollified by China's prosperity, delighted by the return of Hong Kong, and ecstatic at the PLA's possession of some of the most modern weapons in the world.

Mao would also be reassured by the continuation of the "people's proletarian dictatorship," even after 20 years of "reform." Chinese society, in many important respects, continues to be dominated by the Party-state. The centralized power structure of the PRC, with power deriving ultimately from control of the military, concentrated in the hands of a few persons, and wielded without significant institutional constraints, remains intact. The penal code continues to be used to maintain the Communist Party in power, and large-scale political and religious persecutions continue to maintain the muscular tone of the system. The Party-state continues to regard the people as its property, and so they remain subjects rather than citizens.

The official ideology of communism is in headlong retreat, to be sure, but this does not constitute a fundamental threat to the current array of power holders. Because communism was always just an updated version of Chinese autocracy, its death will leave these autocratic traditions intact. Even if the Party were formally to renounce communism tomorrow in favor of, say, a new identity as "social democrats," the traditional pattern of state-society relations would continue, although a new legitimating ideology would of course be required in order to persuade the people to "obey of their own free will."

GREAT HAN CHAUVINISM

The problem for China's leaders is that almost no one, even within the Party, subscribes any longer to the communist myth that the state is temporarily, on behalf of the people, exercising powers that will ultimately "wither." Even the leaders sound at times like skeptics. With the rationale for one-party rule rapidly ebbing away and its foundation of raw force increasingly exposed to public view, a frantic search for alternative sources of legitimacy is underway. In part this involves relentlessly pushing economic development and reducing government interference in the economic lives of the populace. But mostly it involves stoking the fires of nationalism with whatever fuel happens to be at hand, such as the accidental bombing of a PRC embassy during the Kosovo air campaign, or reflections on the lost glories of Imperial China and Confucianism. There is a measure of desperation in all this. After all, it wasn't so long ago that China's past was violently rejected by the late Chairman Mao Zedong, who sought during the Cultural Revolution to erase every last wisp of Confucian thought from the Chinese mind. Yet it was the Sage himself who said that the first task of any government is "to rectify the names" in order to view the world in proper perspective.

The keepers of state orthodoxy, as a substitute for communism, have lately seized upon what I think of as Great Han Chauvinism *(Dazhonghuajuyi):* a potent and peculiarly Chinese combination of nationalism, ultrapatriotism, traditionalism, ethnocentrism and culturalism. Expressions of ultranationalism can

be found in official and semiofficial publications alike. For example, Yuan Hongbing writes, "The renaissance of the China Spirit
[Zhonghua jingshen] will be as a chiming of the morning bell of
the Pacific age. All glory belongs to Great China [weidade
Zhonghua]. The future belongs to the modernized China Spirit—
in the name of the new century!"[21] If Eastern European Communists
saved themselves following the collapse of the Berlin Wall by
becoming "social democrats," then post-Tiananmen Chinese
Communists hope to save their one-party system—China's new
Great Wall against democratization—from collapse by becoming
Great Han Chauvinists. As China's current crop of Legalists tries
to replace the decaying myth of communism with a robust, race-
based chauvinism, the vanguard of the proletariat is reinventing
itself as the protector of the Great Han Race, its culture, and its
traditions.

The Chinese Communist Party has always portrayed itself as
the paramount patriotic force in the nation, but following the
Tiananmen debacle it desperately sought to shore up its crum-
bling mythology by all the institutional means under its control.
The educational system was mobilized to teach students about
China's "history of shame"; state-run factories required their workers to sit through patriotic indoctrination sessions; and the state-
controlled media as well as the schools promoted Chinese
exceptionalism through what is called "state-of-the-nation education," or guoqing jiaoyu.

The official Party definition of guoqing (literally "national situation") is that "China is a nation that has successfully established
a socialist system that over time has proved superior to capitalism but that, nonetheless, requires further political and economic
reform. . . . China has an ancient history that has given birth to
numerous positive national traditions and traits. The negative
ideological influence of the old society, however, has not been
entirely eradicated." Only the Chinese Communist Party, the not-
so-subliminal message ran, could provide the strong central government required by China's unique guoqing and current national
priorities, along with continued economic growth and the means

to recover Chinese preponderance in Asia and accomplish the "rectification of historical accounts" (i.e., revenge on the imperialist powers).[22]

These efforts achieved a bureaucratic apogee in September 1994 with the publication of a sweeping party directive, "Policy Outline for Implementing Patriotic Education."[23] Within the schools, the Party ordered that "Patriotic education shall run through the whole education process from kindergarten to university . . . and must penetrate classroom teaching of all related subjects." While PRC history textbooks have always stoked nationalist fervor and xenophobia, these same attitudes were now to be inserted into everything from beginning readers to junior high school social science textbooks to high school political education classes. The resulting kindergarten-through-college curriculum has been custom designed to breed young patriots.

A second-grade reader includes the story of a young cowherd who "led the Japanese devils into an ambush" by the Communist Eighth Route Army during the Second World War, sacrificing her own life in the process. Another primer, "Ten Must-Knows for Elementary School Students," issued to commemorate the fiftieth anniversary of the People's Republic of China, cites "one hundred years of Chinese people opposing foreign aggression" as the raison d'être for the country's founding. An eighth-grade social science textbook begins, "Our motherland in history was once an advanced and great nation . . . but after the invasions of the European and American capitalist Great Powers, a profound national crisis occurred."

Complex historical events are twisted to fit a simple morality tale of good Chinese patriots versus evil foreign imperialists. Neither the Manchus nor the Nationalists are praised for avoiding outright colonization, only condemned for the insults to China's greatness that occurred on their watches. The Taiping Rebellion, a mid-nineteenth-century uprising with Christian roots that sought to overthrow Manchu rule, is transmogrified into "the largest peasant war in Chinese history," put down by "foreign and Chinese reactionary forces." The Boxer Rebellion, in which a fin-de-siècle secret society brutally killed missionary families and besieged foreign embassies, is venerated as "the high point of the struggle to oppose imperialistic aggression."

"History is a maiden, and you can dress her up however you wish," the Chinese say. The Patriotic Education policy is less about accurately depicting past events than about propagating a meta-narrative designed to stir up the blood of young Chinese. It goes like this: The Middle Kingdom's centuries of national grandeur were ended by foreign imperialists, at whose hands the Chinese people suffered a hundred years of humiliation; but now, under the strong leadership of the Chinese Communist Party, the Chinese are reasserting their traditional place in the world.

The rewriting of history in China is nothing new. In imperial times, every dynastic founder was at pains to commission a warts-and-all history of the previous dynasty. By elaborating in excruciating detail how the previous ruling house had lost the Mandate of Heaven, the new ruler bolstered his own claim. But now, fifty years after the founding of the PRC, the potted histories of the present leadership have a slightly different purpose. They are designed not so much to delegitimate the preceding Nationalist regime, as to create a world view that justifies the recovery of lost Chinese lands and the undoing of the imperialist powers that occupy them.

What this patriotic education comprises, in broad strokes, is a kind of Chinese *Mein Kampf*. The Chinese, it suggests, are a great race which for millennia has rightly dominated its known world. But the foreign imperialists humbled us, tearing off and devouring living parts of the Chinese race and nation, even threatening the whole with disunity. But China has now stood up and is fighting back, determined to recover her lost grandeur no less than her lost territories. We must be wary of things foreign, absorbing only those which make us stronger and rejecting those, like Christianity and Western liberalism, which make us weaker. The first duty of the Chinese state is therefore to nationalize the masses and resist these foreign ideas. Only the Chinese Communist Party has the will and determination to lead the struggle. The new China must gather within its fold all the scattered Chinese elements in Asia.

A people that has suffered a century and a half of Western humiliation can be rescued by restoring its self-confidence. To restore the Chinese nation, the PLA must become modernized and invincible. The world is now moving towards a new millennium, and the Chinese state must see to it that the Chinese race is ready to assume its proper place in the world.[24]

The Party-controlled media have seconded this educational curriculum with a drumbeat of propaganda about the Chinese people and their past designed to appeal to Chinese pride, fan the fires of nationalism, and bolster the Party's own flagging image by identifying it with potent nationalistic symbols. For this program they have found a receptive audience. In a 1994 poll, young people ranked "patriotism" second only to "self-respect" in importance among a list of values. Workers, farmers and science students ranked "patriotism" in first place, up from fifth place a decade ago.[25]

Some aspects of Great Han Chauvinism are merely silly, as when the government churns out propaganda reports claiming that China was first in everything from the use of knives and forks (which later gave way to chopsticks) to golf and tulip cultivation. But the Party-state has much more serious purposes in mind as well, chiefly its own survival. The point of encouraging patriotism, in the words of the "Policy Outline for Implementing Patriotic Education," is "the invigoration of the spirit of the nation, the enhancement of national cohesion, the establishment of national self-respect and pride, *as well as the strengthening and development of the broadest possible patriotic national front*" (italics added). What this means in practical terms, to quote Sinologist Geremie Barme, is "the rearticulation of national-racial icons like the Yellow Emperor and the 'Chinese race,' *Zhonghua minzu*, to define ultra-Chinese sensibilities, as well as debates about the shape of a future Chinese commonwealth." The Party is the self-proclaimed rallying point of the new "patriotic national front," and hopes thereby to make itself indispensable in the eyes of its citizens.[26]

Chinese intellectuals have always had a suppliant, even sycophantic attitude towards the state. Even today, they seem to give in all too readily to the notion of "my state, right or wrong," according to which any action can be justified by a cultural-historical-racial appeal to unity. An example of the symbiosis between those who rule and those who think is *China: Just Say No!* Written by five young intellectuals of the sort who just a few years earlier would have been demonstrating in Tiananmen Square, this tract urges the Chinese people to resist the American "conspiracy" to keep China from assuming its rightful place in the world. In his preface to this popular book, author He Peiling writes that

> the direction that China—as the single existing socialist superpower—will take has become the focus of the world's attention. The U.S., because of deep-rooted ideological differences and its intention to dominate the world all by itself, views China's ascendance with considerable anguish and concern. From [the U.S.] perspective, China might well become a rival that can deter the global hegemony of American culture, economy and military power. Therefore, a conspiracy from the "free world" that is aimed at China has begun to take shape. . . . In sum, the basic policy of the U.S. is the containment of China. The U.S. has already launched a new cold war aimed at China.

Like all books published in the PRC, *China: Just Say No!* could not have appeared in print without an official imprimatur.[27]

The patriotism of ordinary Chinese people verges on jingoism. When the negotiations over the return of Hong Kong to Chinese sovereignty stalled in 1983, China's state-owned film studios produced a patriotic blockbuster called *The Burning of the Summer Palace,* an account of the Anglo-French expeditionary force that in 1860 looted and torched the Jesuit-designed palace of the emperor. The obvious intent was to arouse the Chinese against the reprobate English, who were stubbornly refusing to hand over their ill-gotten gains in South China, specifically Hong Kong. In truth the authorities need not have bothered to inflame public opinion. The surge of Great Han triumphalism that accompanied the recovery of Hong Kong required very little fanning by the state-owned media. In the popular mind, one more historical wrong was being righted, one more imperialist power was paying down its historical debt.

That the people of Hong Kong did not seem to share their enthusiasm passed without note.

Following the accidental bombing of the Chinese embassy in Belgrade, the official propaganda machine turned up the anti-American rhetoric to a white heat. "Evildoers Doomed to Meet Destruction," read one headline in the *People's Daily*, the voice of Party orthodoxy, which went on to compare America's supposed efforts to dominate the world with those of Nazi Germany. The bombing of the embassy was a deliberate attack, the paper charged, a shot across the bow of an increasingly powerful China warning her not to challenge American hegemony. But the Chinese people are aware of America's "vicious" intentions, and will work hard to "build up [China's] national strength and beef up its competitiveness."[28]

These seeds of hate fell on fertile ground. The vast majority of the Chinese people, predisposed by decades of anti–"foreign imperialist" propaganda to believe that the West is always trying to keep China down, saw the attack as intentional. They refused to believe the attack was a "mistake" and rejected NATO's apology, claiming instead that their embassy had been deliberately targeted because China was vigorously denouncing "U.S. hegemonism." The *Beijing Youth Daily* reported that a public opinion survey found that *every one* of the 831 people polled believed America had carried out the bombing deliberately. A majority of fifty-six percent said they thought America was "barbaric and crazy," while thirty-seven percent averred that the U.S. government was "controlled by Nazis."[29]

THE HEGEMON REARMED

China's brand of xenophobia and nostalgia for lost empire would be of only academic interest in Syria or Cambodia; but the People's Republic is no paper tiger. Already the dominant economic power in continental Asia, it is rapidly building up a first-rate military machine. China's military spending is increasing at a double-digit clip, enabling the People's Liberation Army to rapidly expand its arsenal of state-of-the-art nuclear and conventional weapons. This growth is especially alarming in view of decreasing American (and

French and German and Russian, etc.) military budgets and the absence of a credible military threat to China's territory. China is the only major country in the world that is currently undertaking a major military expansion.

As chairman of the Central Military Commission from 1980 on, Deng moved to create a more professional People's Liberation Army.[30] After the expeditionary force was bloodied by the Vietnamese in 1979, he retired the PLA's superannuated generals and promoted more technologically astute replacements. He reduced the number of military regions from eleven to seven, the better to reflect China's strategic goals. And he changed the PLA's order of battle away from the simple rifle companies of the 1940s to include armor and other advanced weapons systems. To acquire militarily useful technology, such as space tracking, nuclear energy, and lasers, he launched a sweeping effort called the "863 Program."[31] Following the collapse of the former Soviet Union, he approved the first purchases of Russian-made high-tech equipment.

Jiang Zemin has turned out to be even more of a booster of PLA modernization than his patron. He has spent billions acquiring arms from Russia. Instead of just continuing the 863 Program, he aggressively expanded it in 1996 into the "Super-863 Program." And he has not only reaffirmed but codified Deng's view that military modernization is the chief object of the modernization of the overall economy.[32]

This "guns before butter" approach is contained in what is called the "Sixteen-Character Policy." Approved by Jiang and the CCP in 1997, the sixteen characters comprise four sentences of four characters each:

- *Ping-zhan jiehe* (Combine peace and war).
- *Junpin youxian* (Give priority to military products).
- *Yi min yang jun* (Let the civil support the military).

As the congressional Cox Report confirms, "the CCP's main aim for the civilian economy is to support the building of modern military weapons and to support the aims of the PLA." What this suggests is a *conscious* effort to manage the growth of China's civilian economy, particularly its technological and industrial capabilities, so as to provide the essential components for the production of modern weapons systems, as well as to use commercial profits to import advanced weapons systems from abroad. The PRC's pursuit of "comprehensive national power" is a three-legged race in which the first two legs—the promotion of high-tech industries and robust economic growth—are tied to the third and key leg: military modernization.[33]

The PRC loudly and publicly denies, with an air of injured innocence, that it holds military modernization to be all-important. In fact the official Beijing line, which has remained unchanged since the late seventies, is that the PRC is devoting the lion's share of its resources to economic development, with military modernization subservient to that goal. The rest of the world can relax.

When talking among themselves, however, many PLA leaders and PRC scholars openly insist on the primacy of military modernization efforts. General Liu Huaqing, for example, former vice-chairman of the CCP's Central Military Commission and member of the Standing Committee of the Politburo, stated in 1992 that economic modernization was dependent not only on "advanced science and technology," but also on "people armed with it." Anything else was "empty talk."[34]

"When you wish to do battle, make it appear that you do not," advised Sun-tzu, whose views continue to be popular in China today, especially among the military. According to the official defense budget, the PRC spent less than $10 billion in 1998—$9.8 billion to be exact—maintaining an army of 3 plus million men, major foreign weapons procurement programs, extensive weapons production facilities, and ambitious research and development efforts. Most informed observers believe this is risible and estimate that real military spending is from four to ten times the amount claimed.[35] This would mean that in 1998, for example, the PRC spent not a paltry $9.8 billion but a robust $39 to $98 billion on its military.

The reason for this huge disparity is out-and-out deception.

The official defense budget only covers basic training, troop pay, and operations and readiness (O&M) expenses. Other military expenditures—everything from military-related research and development, nuclear weapons programs, special weapons procurement, and major arms imports, to expenses associated with the People's Armed Police (PAP) and PLA Reserves, military pensions, and subsidies for defense industries—are hidden away in other parts of the PRC's State Budget or in provincial budgets. In addition, the PLA has several other sources of revenue not included in the official military budget, such as agricultural production on PLA farms, earnings from overseas arms sales, and earnings, now dwindling, from non-military-oriented PLA economic activities.[36]

One thing is certain: China's rapid economic expansion has enabled an equally rapid expansion in its military budget. Since 1992 China has enjoyed phenomenal economic growth, with the GNP increasing at a rate of between eight and twelve percent per year. With the Chinese economy doubling in size every six to nine years, Beijing has an ever larger economic base from which, in the words of the Sixteen-Character Policy, to "let the civil support the military." During the late 1990s, the PRC admits, official military spending increased at a double-digit pace, faster than any other part of the budget. All indications are that China's hidden spending has kept pace.

Since labor costs—a large part of most defense budgets—are so low in China, this money goes a lot further in the PRC than it would elsewhere. Using price parity ratios calculated by the World Bank, for instance, the U.S. Arms Control and Disarmament Agency estimated that the comparable Western value of Chinese military expenditures in 1991, officially only $6 billion, was actually around $51 billion, making the PRC that year the third largest defense spender in the world. Nicholas Kristof argued in the mid-nineties that, corrected for hidden spending and purchasing power, a Chinese defense budget of $6 billion translated into as much as $90 billion in Western spending. A similar adjustment today would yield a figure around $150 billion. China's military spending dwarfs that of other Asian countries, and in all likelihood is second only to that of the United States.

These increases in military spending are being driven by a fundamental shift in strategic doctrine called, with an indirectness Suntzu would have admired, "active defense." After decades in a fundamentally defensive posture, China is now readying its forces to go on the offensive. Its air, sea, and amphibious forces are being outfitted with a wide array of state-of-the-art conventional and nuclear weapons to enable them to deliver a punch far beyond China's borders. Many of these weapons systems are targeted against the U.S. and its forces.[37]

PLA Air Force—The new air force weapons program focuses on power projection and includes at least six kinds of tactical aircraft, aerial refueling tankers, and heavy transport planes. More than fifty Su-27s have already been purchased from Russia with two hundred more to be either purchased outright, or produced indigenously under license, by 2012. Equipped with advanced radar and AA-11 radar-guided missiles capable of hitting targets beyond visual range, these fighters are designed to give China air superiority. The Chinese are also building their own F-10 multirole fighter, due out in 2005, a variation of which may be carrier-deployed. Other known aircraft include an advanced fighter with radar-evading stealth characteristics, a new FB-7 light strike aircraft, an improved F-8 interceptor, and the FC-1, a light fighter based on the MiG-21 that is being developed for the export market.

Using in-flight air refueling kits obtained from Russia, five B-6 bombers have been converted into aerial refueling tankers in an effort to extend the range of Chinese aircraft to cover much of the western Pacific, allowing them, in the words of one Pentagon intelligence report, "to perform some long-range escort, air-to-air, and ground attack missions over the South China Sea or elsewhere in the region."[38] China has also purchased ten IL-76 Russian heavy cargo planes, which provide the lift capacity needed to move men and materiel quickly outside of its borders. As with all Russian weapons, this purchase will enable China, through reverse engineering or direct design assistance, to build its own heavy transports in the future.

The significance of all this hardware is underlined by the PLA

Air Force's recent shift from a defensive strategic doctrine to one that emphasizes taking the offensive.[39]

PLA Navy—As Russia recedes on the threat horizon—so much so that its role has shifted from China's antagonist to its chief supplier of modern arms, a sort of arsenal of totalitarianism—Beijing has become especially aggressive on the maritime front. After decades of languishing as a coastal defense force, the PLA Navy has begun laying down the keels of new warships at a vigorous pace. The PLA Navy has unveiled new classes of destroyers, frigates, and light attack craft; introduced new nuclear attack and ballistic missile submarines, better surface-to-surface and surface-to-air missiles and submarine hunting gear; and added long-range supply ships for landing forces. With the acquisition of the Minsk from Russia, China now has its first aircraft carrier, and a second may be on the way.

China is adding rapidly to the two Luhu-class guided-missile destroyers and five Jiangwei-class guided missile frigates now in its fleet. Even more troublesome is the recent purchase from Russia of two Sovremenny-class destroyers. Pentagon officials believe that the acquisition of the Russian destroyers, part of a total weapons purchase worth $8–10 billion, was a direct response to the deployment of U.S. aircraft carrier task forces during the Taiwan missile crisis of 1996. The Russian destroyers are armed with SS-N-22 Sunburn cruise missiles, designed to strike at the U.S. Aegis-class guided missile warships that form a protective screen of escorts around U.S. aircraft carriers.[40]

China's purchase of four new Kilo-class attack submarines provides it with another carrier-busting weapon. The Russian submarines have been upgraded to be among the quietest diesel submarines in the world, and come equipped with a weapons package that includes both wake-homing and wire-guided acoustic homing torpedoes. The wake-homing torpedo is designed to ignore acoustic ship defense and evasive maneuvers and has been described by the Office of Naval Intelligence (ONI) as especially effective. These same advanced torpedoes and quieting technology will also be deployed on China's new nuclear attack submarines, the Type 093, the first of which will join the PLAN submarine fleet soon after the year 2000. The Type 093 will also carry anti-submarine warfare missiles and anti-ship cruise missiles, reportedly an improved version of China's C801 (itself reverse-engineered from the French Exocet anti-ship cruise missile).[41]

According to the ONI, China is also building a new ballistic missile submarine, the Type 094, in accordance with its "long-term national goal of attaining a survivable nuclear retaliatory force." By far the largest Chinese submarine ever built, it will be armed with sixteen JL-2 missiles, each with a range of 4,000 miles. When deployed early this decade, the ONI report states, "this missile will allow Chinese SSBNs [ballistic missile submarines] to target portions of the United States for the first time from operating areas located near the Chinese coast." This is in addition to China's existing Xia-class ballistic missile submarine, which carries twelve CSS-N-3 nuclear missiles. By 2010 China will have ten nuclear submarines, the ONI estimates, including three new ballistic missile submarines. Add to this approximately forty-five diesel-powered boats, including several submarines of a new type, and China will have by far the largest submarine force in Asia.

Missile Forces—To project force even further afield, China is rapidly expanding its strategic nuclear missile force. China is developing and will soon deploy several new types of intermediate- and long-range ballistic missiles, all of which threaten all or part of the American homeland. A new version of its existing CSS-4 is being deployed, this one with an 8,000-mile range. China is eager to field a road-mobile nuclear missile, which it first tested in 1995 and will soon deploy. Similar in design to the Russian SS-25, these new ICBMs can be shuttled about on Chinese roads and easily hidden. China's missile force also includes more than seventy medium-range nuclear missiles. The new DF-31, with a range of 5,000 miles, will be deployed on mobile launchers and submarines. Another new missile, the DF-41, with a range of up to 7,500 miles, is ready to go into production.

China has also dramatically stepped up production of short-range M-9 and new CSS-X-7 missiles, most of which are aimed at Taiwan. A secret Pentagon intelligence report of January 1999 estimated that

China had already deployed 150 or so missiles along its southeast coast opposite Taiwan by 1998, and predicted that this number would increase to six hundred by 2005.[42] Given that only fifty or so would be required to shut down Taiwan's major airfields, ports, and other strategic assets, these actions more than meet the generally accepted definition of "overkill."

China is also buying or building (with Russian help) advanced Russian surface-to-air missile systems. These include an estimated one hundred of Russia's long-range SA-10s, to be deployed around key government and industrial complexes, and the Russian version of the Stinger anti-aircraft missile, the SA-7. China is known to be working on ways to detect and kill radar-evading stealth aircraft and cruise missiles, which are, as Bill Gertz has written, "systems owned exclusively by the United States."[43]

China's currently accepted inventories of missiles, planes, tanks, and ships, as impressive as these are, must be regarded as minimums, perhaps in some cases fractions, of the real numbers.[44] The PRC is a determinedly evasive opponent, and is hardly going to line up its new SU-27s wingtip to wingtip on the tarmac for U.S. spy satellites to see. Counting the weapons of Sun-tzu's disciples, who believe as an article of faith that "all warfare is based on deceit," requires a more complex calculus. Just as the PRC buries billions of dollars of military spending in other budgets, so we must assume that the PLA is undertaking a similar effort to disguise its assets. Such a shell game would be especially effective for smaller weapons systems, such as short- and medium-range missiles, where the presumption of a multiplier should be operative.

China's willingness and ability to spend huge sums of money on armaments, combined with what the Cox Report called "its insatiable appetite" for military technology and advanced weapons systems, have made it the dominant power in the region, and behind only the U.S. and Russia in global strength. It not only possesses the region's only significant nuclear arsenal and by far the largest number of men under arms: its air force and navy are numerically dominant and becoming more so. China's growing force projection capacity is sending tremors through Asia.

PLA CORRUPTION OR BUSINESS AS USUAL?

It is often said that the rearming of the Hegemon will be hampered
by widespread corruption and a shortage of first-rate military technology. It's true that the PLA has gone into business in a big way,
and this has in turn given rise to a certain amount of corruption.
In one celebrated case, a regimental commander rented out all of
his military license plates to private truckers, whose trucks could
then pass along China's toll roads as "military vehicles," avoiding the frequent tolls.[45]

But those who say that corruption has significantly diminished
the PLA's fighting ability or impeded its military modernization are
exaggerating.[46] And those abuses that do exist are being corrected.
Moreover, much of what might appear to an outside observer as
"corruption" appears routine in the Chinese context. From the
beginning, the Red Army sought to minimize its logistics "foot-
print" on the people by making PLA units responsible for their own
food supply and other material needs. Unlike the Nationalists, who
during the heat of the civil war requisitioned what they needed from
the civilian population, sometimes without paying or even asking, the Red Army was taught to be polite to the civilian population and self-reliant. Once permanent base areas had been
established, PLA troops were put to work planting and harvest-
ing grain crops. Later, after the establishment of the PRC, they
set up their own factories to produce clothes, supplies, and weapons.
With the economic reform, they began to sell some of these goods
on the civilian market; but this represented a natural extension
of their economic activities, not a sharp—and corrupting—break
with the past.

Even with ample funds and strict controls on corruption, the
PRC would take decades to modernize its military without access
to modern weapons systems and military technology from abroad.
Recognizing this, the PLA has gone on a global shopping spree, out-
stripping countries in Europe and the Middle East to become the
world's biggest licit (and illicit) importer of arms and related technology. The F-10 indigenous fighter jet is reportedly based on U.S.
technology illicitly supplied to China by Israel from its cancelled
Lavi fighter program.[47]

Russia has become China's chief supplier of modern weapons and military technology. Virtually all of the weapons technology of the former Soviet Union, including its most advanced systems, is now for sale to the highest bidder—which has turned out to be China. Among other things, Russia has reportedly sold China control and guidance systems from the SS-18 and SS-19 intermediate-range nuclear missiles.[48]

Thanks to the Russian connection, China can leapfrog over obsolete intermediate technologies, developing state-of-the-art military capabilities comparable to those of the U.S. in a decade or less. In the not-too-distant future they will be producing sophisticated weapons systems domestically. The recruitment of Russian scientists, technicians, and engineers, carried out under both official and "unofficial" auspices, is a key part of China's strategy. The five-year Sino-Russian military cooperation agreement, signed in November 1993 by Defense Ministers Chi Haotian and Pavel Grachev, reportedly covered not only weapons sales but also cooperation in personnel exchanges, training, intelligence information-sharing, and mutual logistics support. Private recruitment of unemployed Russian scientists, technicians, and engineers to work in China's military-industrial complex is proceeding apace. There are at present an estimated 10,000 Russian specialists working to help modernize the PRC's military-industrial complex, and the number is growing.

China's efforts to recover its traditional place in the world also drive it to engage in espionage, particularly against the U.S., whose technology is the envy of the world. This effort is spearheaded by PLA General Ding Henggao, who heads China's Commission on Science, Technology, and Industry for National Defense (COSTIND), which oversees development of China's weapons systems and is responsible for identifying and acquiring information, telecommunications and other technology applicable to military use. General Ding, writing in the Summer 1994 issue of *Chinese Military Science,* asserted that "we must study defense-commercial dual-purpose technology and possible transfers from commercial technology to defense use [in order] to make quick advances [in

military development]. . . . We should seize every favorable opportunity to import advanced technology from abroad." Ding also
applauded the opportunities for dual-use technology transfer that
arise from the "increased mutual infiltration" of commercial joint
ventures with the West.

The launch of American communications satellites by Chinese
ballistic missiles is a classic example of General Ding's dictum at
work. On February 15, 1996, a Long March missile exploded upon
take-off, destroying the Intelsat communications satellite, owned
by Loral and Hughes, that it was carrying. An investigation into the
launch failure by engineers from the two U.S. corporations followed,
uncovering an electrical problem in the flight guidance system,
among other troubles. Apparently in violation of U.S. law, detailed
recommendations for correcting these problems and improving
the launch reliability of the Long March were handed over to
Chinese officials. A May 1996 classified study of the incident by
the Air Force's National Air Intelligence Center confirmed that
"United States national security has been harmed."

Following the modifications suggested by Loral and Hughes, the
once notoriously unreliable Long March booster, which Beijing has
in the past used to threaten American cities, has not had a single
mishap. Thus were "commercial joint ventures," in General Ding's
words, used to "transfer commercial technology to defense use"
in order to "make quick advances" in China's military capabilities,
namely, improving the reliability of the nuclear-tipped ICBMs it
has aimed at the U.S.

A shocked House of Representatives in 1998 formed a special
bipartisan committee, headed by Congressman Christopher Cox
of California, to assess the damage done to U.S. national security
by the Loral/Hughes actions. Investigators soon discovered that,
as bad as the transfer of missile technology had been, this was only
a relatively minor part of a much larger problem: a massive Chinese
espionage effort extending over two decades dedicated to the acquisition of U.S. weapons technology. "I can tell you today that
national security harm did occur," a sober Cox reported to a
December 30, 1998, press conference. While much of the Cox

Committee's 852-page report is still classified, what has been made public shows that China's spying has accelerated its weapons development program by fifteen years, cutting the U.S. technology lead in key technologies by half or more.

It was Chinese take-out at the U.S. nuclear weapons laboratories at Los Alamos, Lawrence Livermore, and elsewhere. "The Chinese penetration was total," one CIA official was quoted as saying. "They are deep, deep into the lab's black programs." The most serious thefts, according to the Cox Report, involved design information on "seven thermonuclear warheads, including *every* currently deployed thermonuclear warhead in the U.S. ballistic missile arsenal" (italics added).

Even the most sophisticated warhead the U.S. has ever built, a miniaturized, tapered bomb designed to fit inside the Trident's submarine-launched ballistic missile, is no secret to the Chinese. Nor is Multiple Independently Targeted Reentry Vehicle technology (MIRVing technology for short), which enables such miniaturized warheads to be delivered to different targets.[49] Were China's twenty-four ICBMs all retrofitted with ten miniaturized warheads, the menace to the continental United States would grow tenfold, to 240 warheads. The same technology could be used on the submarine-launched ballistic missiles that China is moving into production.

During the late 1980s, Chinese intelligence operatives infiltrating the Lawrence Livermore National Laboratory obtained secret design data on the enhanced radiation nuclear warhead. The "neutron bomb" kills by deadly radiation, not by a large blast. While the U.S. has never tested it because of pacifist pressures, the Chinese, free from such constraints, have already conducted five tests, sufficient to prove and deploy the weapon.[50]

Encryption technology, vital to the security of the U.S. military's Command, Control and Communications systems, called 3-C systems, may also have fallen into China's hands at the time of the Loral/Hughes fiasco. This technology is one of America's most closely held secrets. Even Australia, a nation allied with the U.S. via the ANZUS treaty, has been denied access to it. Following the explosion of the Loral/Hughes Long March booster on February 15, 1996, U.S. observers were kept from the crash site for five hours—and the highly advanced encryption microprocessor and motherboard were never recovered. The Gulf War alerted the Chinese to the value of information technology, especially satellite encryption, in what is called the "revolution in military affairs." With state-of-the-art encryption technology, Beijing is well on the way to being able, secretly and effectively, to integrate air, land and sea elements in a coordinated attack on, say, Taiwan.

China has also acquired five-axis profiling machines: advanced, computer-controlled machines that can be used to build either ballistic missiles or modern warplanes. By removing excess metal in hard-to-reach places, such machines make aircraft lighter, more maneuverable, and hence more deadly. They were "purchased" by the China National Aero-Technology Import and Export Corporation (CATIC), a branch of the military, from a failing McDonnell-Douglas. The U.S. aircraft manufacturer had been desperate to sign a $1.9 billion contract to manufacture forty passenger aircraft in China, providing Beijing with a perfect opportunity for extortion: Throw in an entire aircraft manufacturing plant, they demanded, or it was no deal. McDonnell-Douglas eventually agreed to sell its entire inventory of five-axis profiling machines from its Columbus, Ohio, plant for a mere $5.9 million, a price the Pentagon later described as a "fire sale." The Pentagon and the intelligence agencies strongly opposed the sale, but it was nonetheless approved in late 1994 by the Commerce Department under the late Secretary Ron Brown. In March 1995 McDonnell-Douglas officials belatedly discovered that "six of the machines had not been sent to the agreed-upon plant in Beijing, but 800 miles away to the Nanchang Aircraft Co.," a facility used to manufacture Silkworm cruise missiles.[51]

The list of weapons technology and equipment stolen by China's agents reads like a PLA wish list. In addition to thefts of MIRVing technology for missiles and encryption technology vital to command and control systems, it includes radio-frequency weapons and radar satellites, missile and military aircraft guidance technology, electromagnetic pulse (emp) weapons technology, and missile design information. By one estimate, the information that China stole saved ten million man-hours of research. What took American scientists fifty years to research and build, took China only a decade to steal and replicate. China's next generation of nuclear warheads and missiles is expected to be modeled closely upon made-in-America technology.[52]

THE HEGEMON LOOKS ABROAD

In 1994 the Defense Department's Office of Net Assessment conducted computerized war games that suggested the PLA would be able to defeat the U.S. military in Asia within twenty-five years. This would put the day of reckoning some time around 2019. The war games could easily become a reality. If the Chinese leadership were interested simply in shifting the strategic balance of power away from the U.S., it would be building missiles of all types—short, medium, and long-range—to overwhelm the Aegis missile cruisers and frigates screening our carriers, and to expose our forward-deployed troops in Korea, Okinawa, and elsewhere to attack. Instead, China is building a blue-water navy and is rapidly modernizing its air force to challenge the U.S. in other ways, and to intimidate its neighbors.

It is no mystery why the PRC is acquiring a full array of offensive weapons that will allow it to project force in mass far from its own borders. Looking abroad, the Chinese see their imperial ambitions constrained by the United States at every point of the compass. Eastward, they see American ground forces in South Korea and Okinawa, and American air force and naval forces in Japan. To the south there is Taiwan, its weapons systems supplied by the United States, whose carriers lurk in the background. Further south are the Philippines, Indonesia and Thailand, with their traditionally close ties to the U.S., while down under are Australia and New Zealand. America has connections in the west as well, in Pakistan and Kazakhstan, although here Chinese influence is on the rise. But still further to the west is NATO, the most formidable alliance the world has ever known. Anchoring the U.S. allies in the Middle East is Israel, surrounded by Egypt, Saudi Arabia, and the emirates. The Eurasian continent, the eastern half of which history and geography have repeatedly awarded to China as vassal and tributary states, is now partly the preserve of the United States.

China is building up its military not so much to assert its prerogatives over other countries in the region, as in anticipation of a contest with the current guarantor of regional security, the United States. The unspoken goal of China's leadership is to break America's back in Asia and thus end America's reign as the sole superpower in the world.

CHAPTER FIVE

The World Map of Hegemony

The size of China's displacement in the world is such that the world must find a new balance in 30 or 40 years. It's not possible to pretend that this is just another big player. This is the biggest player in the history of man.

—Lee Kuan Yew, Singapore, 1994[1]

Those who excel at defense bury themselves away below the lowest depths of Earth. Those who excel at offense move from above the greatest heights of Heaven.

—Sun-tzu, circa 500 B.C.

C hina experts, who have rarely had enough pieces of the infinitely complex Chinese puzzle to accurately forecast China's international behavior, on the whole tend to minimize the possibility of Chinese aggression. They do agree—given the overheated rhetoric coming from Beijing it would be hard not to—that China is bent upon returning Taiwan to the embrace of the motherland and asserting control over the entirety of the South China Sea. But most predict that China's resentment of the U.S. will ultimately subside and that over time it will be content to accept its place in the American-dominated world order.

Yet to assume that the People's Republic of China doesn't have a master plan for the future is not quite correct. The PRC elite have only to look at real maps of historical Chinese empires in order to trace the form of things possible. The Qing dynasty during its eighteenth-century expansionist phase, when China reached its greatest territorial extent, functions as a sort of meta-map. As we discussed earlier, at that time the Celestial Empire ruled a vast territory stretching from the Russian Far East across southern Siberia to Lake Baikal, then southward across Kazakhstan, eastward along the Himalayas, Northern Burma, Laos, and Vietnam. Korea, Nepal, and all of peninsular Southeast Asia acknowledged Chinese suzerainty and paid tribute. It is this map that springs unbidden to the Chinese mind when the shape of a future "Greater China" is discussed.[2] And it is this same map that fires the imaginations of China's present generation of leaders.

It is no accident that as soon as the CCP had control over China Proper, it cast a covetous eye on the one-time Qing dominions. Like the former Soviet Union, which managed to hang on to the Russian Empire while shouting anti-imperialistic slogans, the CCP exempted itself from its own anti-imperialist dogma and sent its armies on the march. The recovery of Tibet and Soviet-occupied border regions in Xinjiang, Inner Mongolia, and Manchuria followed. After a long and frustrating hiatus, Hong Kong and Macao were returned to the embrace of the motherland. Despite these advances, however, Beijing's writ does not yet extend to the fullness of Greater China. And therein lies the problem.

It is sometimes said by its apologists that China has no need to expand because it faces no threat to its territorial integrity. But from Beijing's point of view its territorial integrity *has already been and continues to be violated.* Not only has the island of Taiwan been alienated from the rest of China, so has a vast tier of territories along China's Indian, Central Asia, Mongolian, and Russian borders. From a Sinocentric perspective, all of these territories await "liberation."

The sequence in which these lost territories and tributaries are recovered will be determined by events rather than by master plan. Perhaps this is why the People's Republic of China is aggressively assembling the military capabilities to project power far outside its borders in any direction. An all-azimuth power projection capability will serve China well along whichever point of the compass it encounters weaknesses.

Once the reconstruction of Greater China is complete, the Hegemon may look further afield: intervening in the Middle East, for example, or seeking to estrange Japan from the U.S. The old limits to China's imperial ambitions were set by distance, but contemporary hegemony has no geographical boundaries, only geopolitical ones, which for the moment are determined by America and its European and Asian allies.

China's quest for hegemony may take it through three phases:

- *Basic Hegemony:* The recovery of Taiwan and the assertion of undisputed control over the South China Sea
- *Regional Hegemony:* The extension of the Chinese empire to the maximum extent of the Qing
- *Global Hegemony:* A worldwide contest with the U.S. to replace the current *Pax Americana* with a *Pax Sinica*

BASIC HEGEMONY

Following Nixon's visit to China in 1972, Beijing muted its public saber-rattling over Taiwan for a time. Privately Mao confided to Nixon that it would still be necessary to retake Taiwan by force, confident that this threat would bring Taiwan's leaders to the negotiating table soon after U.S. protection was withdrawn. China pressed for, and received, a withdrawal of U.S. forces from the island and the formal abrogation of the U.S.-Republic of China Mutual Security Treaty. Taiwan's increasing prosperity, however, combined with America's continued willingness to sell it defensive weaponry, kept it from making the expected kowtow.

Communist China's calculations were further upset when Taiwan democratized in the late 80s, and the principal opposition party, the Democratic Progressive Party, began clamoring for a formal declaration of independence. This was a double-edged threat to Beijing, for it meant that not only might Taiwan escape its grasp forever, but the island's peaceful democratization would stand as an embarrassing rebuke to its own authoritarianism.

After a failed attempt to get Taiwan to accept the same formula for reunification that had been imposed on Hong Kong, Beijing started to ratchet up the rhetoric. "If we abandon the threat of force against Taiwan, then it is not possible that peaceful unification will be achieved," President Jiang Zemin told the *Asahi Shimbun* in August 1995, echoing Mao's sentiments of a quarter-century before. To underline his point, the PRC fired several M-9 nuclear capable missiles in the general vicinity of Taiwan.

On the eve of Taiwan's presidential elections in March 1996, China again went ballistic, bracketing Taiwan with M-9 missiles. The PLA went on to rehearse an invasion of the island using amphibious-assault landings, troop-transport drills, helicopter sorties, and artillery firings. Although initially hesitant, President Clinton eventually dispatched two carrier battle groups to Taiwan's offshore waters and sent a warning to Beijing. The Chinese leadership stood down at this show of resolve, but not before its reckless brinkmanship had unnerved the Clinton administration.

China's insistence on the "liberation" of Taiwan, to the point of making this its chief foreign policy goal, gets its emotional edge from a desire to eliminate the last remnants of Chiang Kai-shek's government and army. Until this happens, the CCP elite will not be able to claim that its victory in the Chinese civil war is complete. The Communists are also eager to "liberate" Taiwan for ideological reasons: to contain the spread of the democratic values and institutions that have taken firm root there these past few decades. A democratic and prosperous Taiwan is a dagger aimed at the heart of the one-party dictatorship that is, by fits and starts, attempting to modernize China. From Beijing's point of view, China's two largest dissident groups are the Nationalist and the Democratic Progressive Parties of Taiwan.

Beijing continues to tout as a basis for a cross-strait agreement the "one country, two systems" formula used in Hong Kong. But there is little sentiment on the island for union with China as presently governed. Why would the Taiwanese wish to exchange their newfound freedom for chains forged in Beijing, their locally elected government for a Communist governor, their locally recruited military for occupation by the same army that opened fire on unarmed demonstrators on Tiananmen Square? Neither the

Nationalist Party, which wants unification to proceed only after the mainland democratizes, nor the Democratic Progressive Party, which doesn't want reunification at all, is ready to cede Taiwan's autonomy to Beijing.

China's current policy towards Taiwan is to alternate between threats and negotiations—a variation on the "talk, talk, fight, fight" of the Chinese civil war—a policy calculated to spread panic episodically in Taiwan and break down the morale of the people. Beijing responded to Taiwan President Lee Teng-hui's July 1999 call for "state-to-state" talks by calling him a traitor and announcing that it has the neutron bomb, just in case it needs to pacify a renegade province. While Taiwan is a credible David to the PRC's Goliath, there is little doubt that a determined PLA attack would eventually wear down the island's defenses.[3]

Only the very real possibility of U.S. intervention makes Beijing hesitate. None of Taiwan's neighbors, not even Japan, will lift a hand to help. In 1996 they all politely averted their eyes when missiles came flying through international air lanes and landed in international sea lanes, even though air traffic and shipping were both disrupted. Malaysia and the Philippines quickly declared a policy of neutrality, while the Indonesian foreign minister asserted that the confrontation was purely a Chinese affair. The foreign minister of Thailand went so far as to declare that the Chinese disruption of air and sea travel was "normal."

Since at least the days of Sun-tzu, twenty-four centuries ago, the Chinese way of war has emphasized stealth and deception. In fact, it is hard to imagine a circumstance in which China would formally declare war, unless as a way of demoralizing an already isolated island into preemptive surrender. If the Chinese move against Taiwan, they will do so at a time and in a way that we least expect, perhaps by setting off a high-altitude nuclear burst over the island to disrupt communications, or by suddenly launching a barrage of missiles at key installations.

Such a scenario might seem fanciful if America had not been repeatedly caught off guard in recent years by missile developments in Asia. Iraq, Pakistan, and Iran have all launched short- to medium-range missiles that U.S. intelligence agencies turned out to be embarrassingly unaware that they were even developing. In fact, prior to Iran's July 1998 launch of a missile with an 800-mile range, the CIA had declared that it would be ten years or more before Iranian missiles would be able to target Israel. But Iran hid its missiles from U.S. spy satellites by building them in underground factories. North Korea successfully concealed its missile program in the same way.

It would be surprising, to say the least, if the Chinese leadership were not availing itself of the same obvious tactic to conceal a number of weapons programs. To the missile production lines that we know about should perhaps be added others, buried in underground bunkers, where three shifts of workers a day could be busying themselves in adding to PRC missile stockpiles. Unlike the U.S., the PRC does not publish inventories of its weapons stores in the pages of its national newspapers.

PRC missiles have also become much more deadly, as the difference between the Chinese missile firings of 1995 and 1996 demonstrated. Of the six DF-15 (Dong Feng or "East Wind") missiles fired in July 1995, one had to be destroyed, two went off course, and the remaining three landed several miles away from their targets. By March 1996, thanks to newly purchased Russian missile guidance technology, all four of the missiles fired hit their target areas near the two principal Taiwanese ports of Kaohsiung and Keelung dead on.[4]

"The implications of Chinese missile improvements are ominous for Taiwan," Paul Bracken has written. "Launching forty-five missiles with conventional warheads, China could virtually close the ports, airfields, water works, and power plants, and destroy the oil storage of a nation that needs continual replenishment from the outside world." I believe that the number of missiles required to cripple Taiwan's infrastructure, some of which has been hardened against the dangers of just such an attack, would actually be several hundred. But Bracken's general point stands: As a small island nation, Taiwan is extraordinarily dependent upon its three main ports, four main airports, and handful of major power generating plants to maintain critical services. And whether it takes 45 or 450 missiles to disable them, China will soon be—if it is not already—in possession of the necessary arsenal.[5]

If the new missile guidance systems perform as advertised, there will be minimal civilian casualties, greatly reducing the likelihood of a strong military reaction from the U.S. China will also attempt to tie our hands with the threat of long-range missiles, asking again (as it did in 1996) whether America is willing to sacrifice Los Angeles for Taipei. (Perhaps Angelenos will be treated to missile splashdowns off of Santa Catalina, as Beijing seeks to leave no doubt about its capabilities.) Ruthlessness is a great equalizer. Whatever the U.S. lead in missile technology and numbers of warheads, China outpaces the U.S. in two key ways: a willingness to sustain casualties in war and a readiness to annihilate the enemy, military and civilian, indiscriminately.

As far as timing is concerned, the likelihood of China moving against Taiwan increases with the level of domestic unrest and could be triggered by anything from a general economic slowdown (such as China experienced in 1998–99), to massive layoffs from inefficient state-owned enterprises, to the continuing crackdown on Falun Gong practitioners.[6] Yet a glance at China's recent history of aggression suggests that its actions are often beyond the realm of such rational calculation. The Sino-Indian War of 1961 might be explained in part by the need to distract the Chinese people from their gnawing bellies, since at the time of that attack, the country was in the grip of a devastating famine that would in the end cost some forty million lives.[7] It is even possible to hypothesize that China's invasion of Vietnam in early 1979 was an effort by Deng Xiaoping to solidify his own grip on power during that difficult transitional period. But what of the show of force against Taiwan in 1996, at a time of relative domestic prosperity and political quietude?

Timing is unpredictable because the Chinese elite practice what might be called the politics of historical revenge. Political and military leaders alike are still conscious of slights that occurred a century or more ago; given almost any pretext, they will seek in some way to avenge them. Neither the Chinese people nor any other institutions within China, such as the National People's Congress, serve as a check on the sudden, seemingly arbitrary act. Indeed, the passionate nationalism of the Chinese, shared by elite and ordinary people alike, is a constant goad in the direction of belligerence in speech and act.

When Taiwan's President Lee Teng-hui suggested in July 1999 that negotiations between Taipei and Beijing should be conducted on a "state-to-state" basis, the *People's Daily* became apoplectic. It didn't matter that President Lee was only restating, a bit more forcefully, Taipei's long-held position that representatives of the two governments should negotiate directly. Beijing, demanding "party-to-party" talks (as in the days of the civil war) called him a "traitor" who was "taking extremely dangerous steps." The PRC ratcheted up the rhetoric just weeks before Taiwan's March 2000 presidential elections, releasing a white paper that bluntly reiterates the Communists' long-standing threat to use force: "If the Taiwan authorities refuse . . . the peaceful settlement of cross-straits reunification through negotiations, then the Chinese government will only be forced to adopt all drastic measures possible, including the use of force."[8] This verbal bullying is typical, and it reinforces a tendency towards aggressive acts. China exists in a political world where the word is father to the deed.

One account of the Taiwan missile crisis of 1995–96 has it that President Jiang's hand was forced by his generals. Jiang was reluctant to threaten Taiwan directly but his generals insisted, or so the story goes. The thought that generals eager to exact revenge on Taiwan's Nationalists for reasons now more than half a century old have their fingers on the firing buttons of China's missiles is an unsettling one. Although this is small consolation, it is just as likely that Jiang agreed wholeheartedly with the proposed action. And the subsequent absence of popular protests in China— the missiles were fired off to general approbation—is a sobering reminder that the public supports its leaders.

Stepping Stones

The Spratlys and the Paracels are island chains hardly worthy of the name. Consisting of a few dozen rock outcroppings each, many of which are underwater at high tide, they lack a source of fresh water and have never been inhabited. What they lack in land area, however, they more than make up in sweep. The Paracels, located equidistant from China, Vietnam, and the Philippines, are hundreds of miles in extent. The Spratly Islands, another five hundred miles further south, stretch across additional hundreds of miles of open ocean between Vietnam, Malaysia, and the Philippines.

China is aggressively moving to take control of the two archipelagos, ignoring the competing claims of a half-dozen other nations. In a December 15, 1998, report to House Republican leaders, Congressman Dana Rohrabacher reported that "the pattern of Chinese naval bases in the Spratlys shows an encircling strategy of the energy-rich islands and an intimidating military presence along the vital sea route that connects the strategic Strait of Malacca with the Taiwan Strait." Some eleven Chinese bases have been detected to date.

China's claims are usually interpreted in economic terms. Indeed, China's already voracious appetite for energy is straining domestic sources, and the continental shelf of the South China Sea is suspected to possess vast oil and natural gas fields. Yet Beijing's efforts to transform the South China Sea into a Chinese lake have strategic reasons as well. The Strait of Malacca is a maritime choke point connecting the Pacific and Indian Oceans; through this vital sea lane passes seventy percent of the crude oil used to fire the economies of Japan, Taiwan, and South Korea. Free passage through the Strait of Malacca is critical to any effective U.S. response to crises in Asia and the Middle East.

From the bases that it is building on Mischief Reef and elsewhere in the Spratlys, Chinese air, naval and marine forces could strike not only at shipping, but at all the countries that surround the South China Sea, including such U.S. allies as the Philippines, Brunei, and Thailand. The intimidation factor of having the PLA as a near neighbor could induce some of these countries to distance themselves nervously from the U.S. Peninsular Southeast Asia now finds itself sandwiched between a Chinese listening post and naval base in Burma, and a growing Chinese presence in the South China Sea.

REGIONAL HEGEMONY: THE SHAPE OF THINGS TO COME

Once Beijing has asserted control over Taiwan and the South China Sea, the Chinese surge could subside—or, the present Chinese dynasty, like its imperial predecessors, may attempt to leverage its very real economic and military clout into regional hegemony.

The "Open Door" policy has ensured not only rapid economic growth within China, but also its economic integration with large parts of East and Southeast Asia in ways whose final impact has yet to be determined. This economic interdependence gives China a strategic interest in maintaining regional stability, to be sure, but also increases its stake in ensuring that China-friendly policies emerge from the region's capitals, as well as in protecting the Chinese minorities whose entrepreneurial skills drive the economies of most Southeast Asian countries.[9]

Among Beijing's most important geopolitical assets must be numbered the sixty million wealthy overseas Chinese, who occupy key economic roles in a dozen Asian countries. These "bridge compatriots," or *qiaobao*, have done extremely well in their adopted countries, most notably in Singapore, Malaysia, Thailand, the Philippines, and Indonesia. In Southeast Asia alone, the aggregate assets of the five hundred leading Chinese-owned companies totaled about $540 billion in 1994. The aggregate income of the sixty million *qiaobao* is, at $500–600 billion, approximately equal to the GDP of the PRC itself.[10] Colonies of wealthy Chinese are to be found in all of China's neighboring countries, from Myanmar (Burma) and Nepal to the Central Asian Republics, Mongolia, and Siberia. Pride in China's resurgent greatness, the advantages to be gained from China's economic growth, and continuing immigration of their compatriots from China helps keep their ethnic identity alive and oriented toward Beijing.

While the European nation-states and their scattered offspring around the world have lost interest in territorial aggrandizement, border disputes continue to form the heart of China's foreign policy. Where existing national boundaries fail to conform to the Qing Empire at its height, they tend to be suspect. The reestablishment of China's regional hegemony in Asia may well result, especially in the north and east, in an attempt to redraw existing borders.

The ideological justification for Beijing's intervention in the affairs of neighboring states is the unquestioned superiority of the Chinese way of life, the flip side of which is the special responsibility that China feels towards the less-favored peoples on its periphery. Even today, the Chinese possess an inordinate sense of their own superiority—over the Tibetans, for example. Jiang Zemin, boasting of the social and cultural benefits that Chinese rule has brought to Tibet, sounds a lot like Rudyard Kipling trumpeting the civilizing mission of the British Empire. And for good reason. While the late-nineteenth-century notion of a "White Man's Burden" has fallen into desuetude, even disgrace, in the West, the idea that there is a "Chinese Burden" to oversee the well-being of neighboring peoples is widely accepted in China at the beginning of the twenty-first century. However anachronistic such sentiments may seem to the Western mind, they continue to inflame the minds of the Chinese—and could easily be enlisted by the Beijing regime to help justify Chinese expansionism.

Sinifying Siberia

It is revealing that senior Chinese leaders in interviews have shown a paternalistic attitude toward all of China's immediate neighbors with the exception—to date—of Russia. Yet Russia is where the major territorial shifts may take place. That Russia has governed the Russian Far East since 1898, and other Asian territories for an even longer period of time, will not deflect China from its designs on those territories. After all, Taiwan has been ruled from China for only five (1945–49) of the last 105 years. If this narrow slice of time is sufficient grounds for the Beijing regime to stake a claim of sovereignty, then other territories lost in the last century or so—like the Russian Far East, parts of Siberia, Mongolia, and parts of Central Asia—can be claimed as well.

Russian designs on the Far East reached their greatest extent immediately following World War II, when Soviet troops occupied Manchuria and Inner Mongolia. Pushed back to the pre-war borders by an insistent Mao, Russia's hold on Siberia appeared unbreakable until 1990. Then came the collapse of the Soviet Union, leaving Siberia far removed from Russia's European heartland. This huge swath of territory from Lake Baikal to the Pacific Ocean, almost as large as Canada, is occupied by only eight million aging Russians, a number that is declining from year to year due to death and emigration. To the south of this vast, nearly empty land wait 1,300 million Chinese.

Better relations between Moscow and Beijing in the eighties brought a flourishing barter trade, with Siberia's raw materials flowing south in exchange for Chinese-made consumer goods. But in the nineties, with the collapse of Soviet border controls, China began to export another product to Siberia: people. Up to half a million Chinese a year are moving across the now-porous border each year, setting up shop in the Russian Far East and Siberia proper. They bring with them their families and children, and live in their own separate Chinatowns. Something like five million Chinese already live on Russian soil. If Chinese don't already outnumber Russians in these areas of cohabitation, they soon will. Russian Defense Minister Pavel Grachev warned in 1995, "The Chinese are in the process of making a peaceful conquest of the Russian Far East."[11] Though complaining about this ingress of illegal immigrants, Russia has not moved to stanch the flow, much less to expel those already in Siberia.

While Russian officials view this tidal wave of immigration with alarm, Beijing seems quietly pleased. The outflow relieves unemployment at home, facilitates trade and, most importantly, strengthens irredentist claims on lands the Chinese once ruled. China's leaders haven't forgotten the machinations of Muraviev who, by deceit and false maps, stole the lands west of the Ussuri a century ago. Nor have they forgotten the earlier treaties that alienated hundreds of thousands of square miles of land north of Manchuria and Mongolia. To them, the Russian conquest of Siberia proper, completed in 1790, seems dismayingly recent, and not at all irreversible. Indeed, the ebb and flow of Chinese history would almost seem to guarantee its reversal. As James Billington, Russian scholar and Librarian of Congress, noted recently, China's irredentist claims, its energy needs, and the Chinese guest worker population in the Russian east "make a Chinese move against Siberia likely in the next ten to fifteen years."[12]

Although Russia remains too powerful militarily for China to challenge directly at the present time, its weakening will tempt China to foster the Russian Far East's increasing economic dependency on the cross-border trade. With Chinese encouragement, this area could slip away from Moscow's grasp and into Beijing's own orbit without any sudden or dramatic break, and without the firing of a shot. Open borders and the quiet encouragement of Chinese emigration (already happening) would then do the rest. Within a generation, Russians would be reduced to a small minority, powerless to resist the clamoring of the Chinese majority for reunification with the motherland. Nearly three million square miles of continental Northeast Asia would belong to China.

Mongolia and the Central Asian Republics

Landlocked between China and Russia, Mongolia was historically Chinese territory until 1921, when the Soviets made it their own puppet state, the Mongolian People's Republic. Having ruled Mongolia for hundreds of years before, China will have no difficulty in resurrecting a claim.

As in Siberia, economic ties across the Sino-Mongolian border are proliferating, while trade between Mongolia and Russia weakens. Similar, too, is the immigration situation, with thriving communities of Chinese traders now prospering in Ulan Bator and other urban areas. If the Russian economy continues to stagnate, Mongolia could become an economic dependency of China. The Chinese government, which only reluctantly recognized Mongolia's independence at Moscow's urging in 1950, may propose a customs union, if not actual reunification, in years to come.[13] Were central authority in Russia to collapse, Beijing would almost certainly move vigorously to assert its historical claim over Mongolia.

When the Central Asian Republics escaped from the Soviet grasp in the early nineties, China's immediate reaction was to try cautiously to make this situation permanent. In April 1996 China signed a joint border and security agreement with Kazakhstan, Kyrgyzstan, Tajikistan and Russia. President Jiang Zemin paid a state visit to Kazakhstan three months later, and assured the Kazakhs that China would support "the efforts made by Kazakhstan to defend its independence, sovereignty, and territorial integrity." Since much of Kazakhstan was wrested from China by the czars, this guarantee of support for Central Asian independence is most likely an attempt to forestall any potential Russian effort to reclaim the region, rather than a permanent renunciation of any territorial ambitions on the part of China.

China is interested in the rich energy resources that these republics contain. Chinese traders are also moving into the region's cities and have become the principal source of consumer goods. If the Russian breakdown continues, however, China could become increasingly assertive in the region, seeking to bring the Central Asian republics completely within its sphere of influence. The rectification of its borders with Kazakhstan could then become an issue.

The Return of the Tributary: The Korean Question

The Korean Peninsula, strategically located between China, Russia, and Japan, is the key to dominating East Asia. North Korea, a hardline Stalinist state with a million-man army, adroitly played China and the USSR against each other in the years of the Sino-Soviet split. The Soviet collapse and subsequent Russian implosion have left Pyongyang looking primarily to Beijing. The North Korean famine of the late nineties would have been worse without the trainloads of grain and oil provided by the Chinese. The No-dong missile could not have flown as soon or as far without the assistance of Chinese missile technology. Were China to recover the Russian Far East, this would permanently close off Pyongyang's Russian option and confirm North Korea as a Chinese tributary.

If the Kim Jong-il regime collapses, Beijing might move troops into the north to establish a puppet regime or, alternatively, to use as bargaining chips in brokering the reunification of the peninsula on its own terms. These terms would likely be a complete withdrawal of American forces from the Korean Peninsula, abrogation of the U.S.-ROK security treaty, and a formal declaration on the part of the new Korean state of its nonaligned status. The withdrawal of U.S. forces by itself would effectively reduce Korea first to neutrality, then to gradual subjugation as a traditional tributary state.

A U.S. withdrawal from South Korea occasioned by other circumstances (renewed isolationism, budget constraints, rising Korean nationalism, etc.) would probably also be succeeded by a Sino-Korean accommodation. The fiercely anti-Japanese sentiments of the Korean people (fully reciprocated by the Japanese) make it unlikely that South Korea and Japan would be able to unite effectively against China. Japan's regional role would be greatly reduced, and the U.S. position in East Asia would become tenuous. If the whole of the Korean Peninsula were to come under Chinese domination, Asian hegemony would be within China's grasp.

Southeast Asia

Southeast Asia, a pendulous bulge hanging from China's underbelly, has traditionally been dominated by China. Today, China's sphere of influence is rapidly expanding. Myanmar, Laos, and Cambodia already follow China's lead. Except for the historically hostile Vietnamese, who even today continue to suffer Chinese military incursions,[14] China's influence in other capitals throughout the region is on the ascent. Driving this process are large numbers of bridge compatriots, common economic interests, and certain characteristics shared by all Asian cultures.

Myanmar is perhaps China's closest ally in the region. The military dictatorship that dominates that country has found in China an uncritical source of arms, aid, and international support. In return, it has provided the Chinese navy free run of port facilities on Myanmar's offshore islands and a listening post on the Indian Ocean. Operating from Myanmar, China can maintain

a naval presence in the Indian Ocean as well as exert strategic leverage on the Strait of Malacca, not to mention Southeast Asia more
generally. The Beijing-Rangoon alliance enables China to bracket
India between two allies, Myanmar and Pakistan, and effectively
thwart New Delhi's regional ambitions in South Asia.

The influence of bridge compatriots can be seen in Malaysia,
where the Chinese comprise roughly a third of the population and
control perhaps two-thirds of Malaysia's economy. Prime Minister
Datuk Mahathir of Malaysia is the most pro-Chinese of the
Southeast Asian leaders, the Myanmar junta aside, and consequently
is the most anti-American. Mahathir's position at a May 1996 forum
in Tokyo on regional security could have been China's: he publicly challenged the need for the U.S.-Japan Security Treaty and
asked to know the name of the enemy the alliance was directed
against. Though he claims that Malaysia does not need allies, he
appears to be closely linking his country's fortunes to China.

Singapore, too, is drawing closer to China. Port visits by the U.S.
Navy are still welcomed, but bridge compatriots control the city-
state's economy and politics, and are increasingly sycophantic where
China is concerned. Singapore has welcomed substantial numbers
of well-heeled mainland Chinese emigrants, whose residence abroad
allows them to take advantage of the five- and ten-year tax holi-
days offered by Beijing to "foreign" investors.

In Thailand, where bridge compatriots control about seventy-
five percent of the economy, there has also been a pronounced
tilt toward China. When the Thai Prime Minister, Chavalit
Yongchaiyudh, visited Beijing in 1997, his purpose was reportedly
to establish a firm strategic alliance with "Greater China." The
Thai elite was said to have "recognized China as a superpower that
has a global role," and to wish for their country to serve as "a bridge
between China and ASEAN."[15] Chinese immigration to Thailand
is relinking that country's partly assimilated Chinese community
(the Chinese have mostly taken Thai names) to its homeland. At
present, Thailand remains a U.S. ally, a country from which the
Voice of America broadcasts into China and where the U.S. Marines
hold their annual Cobra Gold exercises. At the same time, Thailand
is increasingly anxious not to offend Beijing.

GLOBAL HEGEMONY: THE IMPERIAL STRETCH

What would China as a global power look like? Having unified all of the East Asian mainland, it would then try to neutralize America's remaining allies in a way that leads to the expulsion of America from its offshore bases in Asia. It would complete its dominance of Southeast Asia by bringing the Philippines and Indonesia under its sway. To extend its reach further afield, it might seek a temporary alliance with either Russia or Japan, and then attempt to force the remaining state into nonaligned status. It would neutralize India, and extend its reach into the Middle East and Africa. Like the Soviet Union at its height, it might even seek satellites in the Americas.

In the Philippines, bridge compatriots are only two percent of the population but they control roughly half the economy, and Chinese immigration is increasing. The Philippine government is increasingly reluctant to criticize China's actions publicly. The PLA's establishment of a military base on Mischief Reef off the Philippine coast elicited only muted protests. At the same time, the Philippines was quick to apologize to its giant neighbor when a July 1999 collision between a Philippine patrol boat sent a Chinese fishing boat to the bottom. With a Chinese blue water navy dominating the South China Sea and Chinese air force bases a couple of hundred miles offshore, the Philippines might feel compelled to adjust to the new reality of Chinese strength.

Indonesia, which was never part of China's imperial sway, is already worried about being drawn into the Chinese orbit. Its Chinese minority is roughly two percent of the population, but owns ninety percent of the economy and has fairly close economic ties with the motherland. Some in the archipelago find this alarming. Saydiman Suryohadiprojo, who served as Indonesia's ambassador to Japan, warned that "Chinese economic intervention in the region" would draw upon support from local bridge compatriots and could even lead to Chinese-sponsored "puppet governments."[16] China's growing economic and naval strength could lead Indonesia to accept Chinese dominance in the region.

India never had to build a Great Wall, since its northern

approaches are guarded by the highest mountains in the world. During times of dynastic tumescence, Chinese armies marched north or west against the nomads of the Manchurian and Mongolian and Central Asian steppes, or south against the tribal peoples of the tropics; but India was almost unreachable, and so it remained forever outside of China's imperium, even as a tributary state.

Now, however, India and China's relations are no longer benignly determined by geography. A Chinese army advanced into India in 1962 over the same mountain range that once was a nearly impassable barrier. Roads now run right up to the border in several places. Pakistan and Myanmar are now both Chinese allies, neatly bracketing India to the east and west. And the PLA Navy, operating from a new base in Myanmar, has opened a new front on the Indian Ocean. When Congressman Christopher Cox met with Gujral in 1997, the Prime Minister complained about the "pincer movement [that the PRC was carrying out] on India." Gujral "pointed specifically to the deployment of nuclear missiles in Tibet, to the submarines in the Indian Ocean . . . to the fact that Burma had been turned into a PLA armed camp and Pakistan was being armed by the PRC as an irritant to India."[17]

Granted, there are no indications that China actually has designs on Indian territory, and in 1991 the two countries signed a peace treaty resolving—in China's favor—the territorial disputes over which they had gone to war thirty years before. Rather, China's policy seems to be aimed at thwarting India's ambition to become a regional power. The long competition between the world's largest socialist country and the "world's largest democracy" is over, China seems to be saying, and China has won.

Ally with Russia or Japan?

The collapse of Russia's questionable experiment with democracy, perhaps following the election of a communist or a radical nationalist to power, would open the way to a renewed coalition between that country and China. They are already united by common grievances against policies of the "hegemony-seeking" United States, such as the expansion of NATO.[18] Both are attempting to keep pace with the reigning superpower through extensive military cooperation programs. This time around, however, a Sino-Russian axis would be led from Beijing. Its economic basis would be the expansion of trade between the two countries, with China providing consumer goods in exchange for Russian raw materials and industrial products. Its strategic goal would be the ejection of the U.S. from Asia.

A China-Japan coalition, though far less likely, is also possible. A rancorous falling out with the U.S. over trade matters, combined with a growing Chinese market for Japanese-made goods, could lead Japan to reassess its alliance with the U.S. America's unilateral withdrawal from its forward positions in East Asia, perhaps under some notion of ceding China its "natural sphere of influence," could also lead Japan to decide to cast its lot with China.

The result would be a tectonic shift of power. A Sino-Japanese axis would effectively bring together the world's second and third largest economies, creating a co-prosperity sphere roughly equal in size to the U.S. economy. Such a condominium would enjoy some felicitous complementarities as well, combining China's natural resources and manpower with Japanese technology, industry, and financial resources.

How could China turn Japan to its own purposes? Resolving conflicting territorial claims over the Sentaku Islands *(Diao-yu Tai)*, located approximately equidistant from Japan, China, and Taiwan, would eliminate one source of disharmony between the two powers. China could further open up its markets to Japanese-made goods, creating a "pro-China" lobby in Tokyo of Japanese multinationals interested in improved relations. Emphasizing the cultural affinities between the two societies would help to gloss over memories of Japanese aggression in World War II with more positive images of the Confucian culture that dominates the history of both countries.

Such a consortium is admittedly unlikely, and could probably be precipitated only by a full-scale American withdrawal from Asia. Even then, Japan's sense of abandonment and insecurity might lead her not into China's open arms, but rather to undertake a massive rearmament program driven by a Fortress Japan mentality. For China, this is an outcome to be avoided at all costs.

In the event of a Sino-Russian axis, Beijing would urge Japan to keep its military capabilities modest at the same time it nudges Tokyo toward neutrality, perhaps with the argument that a neutral Japan would have greater access to China's markets. President Jiang Zemin has made a point of reassuring visiting Japanese leaders that "China will never intimidate other countries even after it becomes stronger."[19] Beijing would also raise questions about America's staying power in Asia, in an attempt to devalue the worth of the U.S.-Japan Security Treaty in Tokyo's eyes.

Wuwei is No Way

*Today China's economic power makes U.S. lectures
about human rights imprudent. Within a decade it
will make them irrelevant. Within two decades it will
make them laughable.*

—Richard Nixon, 1994[1]

I n suggesting that the U.S. ignore human rights abuses in China, Nixon was retreating, whether he knew it or not, into the Daoist doctrine of *Wuwei*, whose two characters mean literally doing nothing deliberately. Many China experts have followed the former president's lead, arguing that there is nothing to be gained, and much to be lost, by lecturing China. They are so attuned to China's "sensitivities" on human rights that they quail at making a strong case for their observance. In the name of moral equivalence, they set aside China's obviously retrograde political values and institutions. Instead, they propose major U.S. concessions on a whole range of issues in the hope of making minor, incremental improvements in China's behavior which, more often than not, do not materialize.

For Americans, China has always been not so much a country but a state of mind. We have always invested China with our own hopes and illusions and, as these pleasant fantasies become addictive, we have fought against the intrusion of a harsher reality.[2] The latest in the long series of fantasies we have nourished about China is that forces have been unleashed in China that will lead to its peaceful evolution into a free-market democracy regardless of what the U.S. does (or doesn't do). Many lines of argument converge on a single policy point: that we do nothing. *Wuwei* is best way.

The motivations of those who espouse such a belief are complex. American companies who do business in China worry that promoting human rights and democracy in that country will lead the Beijing regime to retaliate, and that their in-country operations will suffer losses as a result. Diplomats prefer to avoid such contentious matters because they give rise to unpleasant encounters. Some foreign policy analysts, including a number of Sovietologists and Sinologists, are advocates of *Wuwei* because they wish to continue playing the China card against Russia (or even against Japan), or fear a backlash from the Beijing regime. Those who have heavily invested their treasure, time, or hopes in China have become, in effect, hostages to Beijing, zealous advocates of a Daoist paradox that goes like this: *China will change only if we don't try to change it.* Thus, they have created a mythology that threatens to determine the course of American China policy.

Myth:
COMMUNISM IS MORIBUND
AND DEMOCRACY IS THE WAVE OF THE FUTURE

This myth was given currency by the remarkable events of the late eighties. Communism around the globe seemed in pell-mell retreat. Forty years into the Cold War, we had reached "the end of history" and the democratic moment had come.

On April 18, 1989, demonstrations began in China, sparked by the death of Hu Yaobang, a former party leader cashiered by Deng Xiaoping and the gerontocrats three years before for being too soft on democracy. Groups of students marched to Tiananmen Square, the symbolic heart of China, and held rallies to denounce corruption, bureaucracy, and dictatorship. As the marches came to include workers along with students, and as their antigovernment tone became more pronounced, the *People's Daily* declared that the students had launched a "conspiracy" to "poison people's minds, create national turmoil and sabotage the nation's political stability." When martial law was imposed on May 20, a million people, young and old alike, took to the streets in protest. The leadership was stunned by the magnitude of the uprising. The first spontaneous mass movement since the founding of the PRC had erupted, seemingly out of nowhere. The global tide of democratization had reached China's shores, and seemed poised to overwhelm the Beijing regime.

The influx of democratic ideas into China during its period of openness to the West was paying off, and more quickly than anyone had imagined. The people of China were looking beyond the present one-party dictatorship, whose misrule they had suffered for decades, to a government that would be respectful of their wishes. Even the brutal crackdown that followed on June 4 was read by many as the lashing tail of the dying dragon.

But by 1991 the dissident movement within China had been crushed. In the years since, a few brave individuals have spoken out from time to time, but no organized opposition exists, or is allowed to exist. The 1999 attempt to form the China Democracy Party was stillborn when its leaders, Wang Youcai and Xu Wenli, were sentenced to eleven and thirteen years respectively. Li Peng, the leader of the National People's Congress, has declared that the Beijing regime "will have zero tolerance" for new parties.[3] The Chinese Democracy and Justice party, with its headquarters in New York, claims to have 5,000 members in China, but is neither visible nor active there.

In retrospect, the high tide of democratic sentiment in China may have been reached in June 1989. The demonstrations were led by a generation of students who were born during the Cultural Revolution, grew up cynical about the CCP and its leaders, and were attracted to America's democratic ideals. They viewed Deng Xiaoping's opening to the West—which meant to America—as their salvation from a moribund economy and an oppressive political system.

The present generation of students is the product of a very different experience. Born after the end of the Cultural Revolution, these children of the economic reform have lived through a period of political stability and double-digit increases in per capita income.[4]

This reform generation are nationalists, having been taught the history of China's humiliation at the hands of the Western powers. They are also Great Han Chauvinists, steeped in the glories of China's imperial past. They are leery of the dangers of "chaos" and do not support any radical change in the status quo, at least over the near term. As howling mobs raged in front of the American embassy following the bombing of the Chinese embassy in Belgrade, I spoke with an American businessman with many years of experience in China. "Ten years ago they were ours," he told me sadly. "Now they are theirs." He meant that the Chinese Communist Party, having successfully waved the bloody shirt of nationalism, had reclaimed its young.

Myth:
THE RISE OF MARKET FORCES AND INTERNATIONAL TRADE WILL TRANSFORM CHINA INTO A FREE-MARKET DEMOCRACY

America has, from the beginning, celebrated China's economic reform. We were pleased to see the Chinese people, for their own sake, begin to shake off the immiseration of communism. The end of the agricultural commune in 1980–81, for example, helped to lift tens of millions of Chinese peasants out of penury. The rise of a class of small businessmen, shopkeepers and traders in the years since has accomplished the same end in the cities. But beyond this, we were convinced that the rise of market forces in China, combined with burgeoning foreign trade, was going to encourage a broad movement for personal freedom, human rights and, eventually, democratic governance. Underlying our optimism was the core American belief that economic and political liberty are indivisible.

The Tiananmen demonstrations seemed to validate this belief. They produced evidence of a convergence of interests between the idealistic students and a new middle class of businessmen. Wan Runnan, an entrepreneur who ran Stone Computers, and Lu Jinghua, a clothing store owner, were among those entrepreneurs who helped to support the demonstrators, providing food and drink, for example, to the students occupying the square.

The massacre was greeted by universal revulsion, but Americans differed on its meaning. Some said that China had never really changed after all, and would not change, without the pressure of trade and other sanctions. Others, including then-President George Bush, generally opposed sanctions because they believed that continued economic reform guaranteed China's democratic prospects. "I believe that China, as its leaders state, will return to the policy of reform pursued before June 3," the president wrote in vetoing a bill to allow Chinese students then studying in the U.S. to remain here. "I further believe that the Chinese visitors [to America] would wish to return to China in those circumstances."[5] In this view, June 4th was merely a blip on the radar screen of China's progress towards a more open society; in the long run, the Beijing regime would not be able to resist the demands for human rights that flowed from the economic reform.

By 1990 the question of revoking China's Most Favored Nation status was being hotly debated. Revoking MFN (or, as it has been called from 1998 on, Normal Trade Relations) would raise average tariff rates on Chinese goods entering the U.S. from four percent to around forty percent, thus slowing the growth of Chinese imports and encouraging companies to site new factories in countries other than China. Groups such as the U.S.-China Business Council, which represents American firms doing business in China, were adamantly opposed to putting conditions on, much less revoking, MFN. Any restrictions on trade with China would slow down the economic reform, they argued, and might jeopardize it altogether. For want of a free market, human rights and democracy would be lost. Perhaps the most sweeping claim for the benefits of open trade was made by Ned Graham of East Gates International, who maintained that "Expanding U.S. economic ties with China will continue to benefit religious organizations working in China by encouraging China's adherence to international law and a rules-based trading system, facilitating China's civil society in developing its rule of law and expanding personal freedoms for its population."[6]

In fact, oppression can, and does, coexist quite comfortably with capitalism. Despite having a free-market economy and adhering to international law and a rules-based trading system, the Republic of South Africa, for instance, practiced apartheid for many decades. The demise of apartheid had far less to do with efforts by U.S. companies to advance human rights in South Africa under the Sullivan principles, than with the rise of a political movement led by a man named Nelson Mandela. Yet American businesses in China are so concerned to preserve good relations with those in power that they reacted with hostility even to the Clinton administration's modest and abortive attempt in 1994 to encourage American businesses to develop a set of standards, comparable to the Sullivan principles, for promoting human rights in China.[7]

That political freedom cannot long exist without economic freedom is demonstrable; but the opposite case—that economic freedom leads inevitably to political liberty—is much weaker, especially in Asia. The countries of Singapore, Indonesia, and Malaysia remain three of the least democratic countries in the region, despite having economies that are generally characterized as free-market. And after more than twenty years of economic reform in China, every major dissident is either in prison or in exile.

The economies of many Asian countries are run by a political-economic elite that specializes in insider trading and sweetheart deals. Crony capitalism, as this is called, creates a political-industrial complex with a stranglehold on important sectors of the national economy. The Suharto family, long-time leaders of the crony capitalist cartel in Indonesia, for instance, were able to profit mightily from their business connections. Their most important allies were Indonesia's Chinese, who control 110 of the country's 140 leading business conglomerates.

Crony capitalism hardly suffices, however, to define the economic practices of China's current ruling elite. Those entrepreneurs who are most successful in China today are related to the founding fathers of the People's Republic of China, the several hundred Party and military leaders who led the PLA to victory in the Chinese civil war. These princelings, as they are called, have cleverly exploited their connections by blood and marriage to the ruling elite. Many have become key intermediaries between major foreign investors and the Chinese government, professional fixers whose family ties help to keep deliveries of raw materials arriving on time and assembly lines running smoothly in return for a share of the profits. Thus is political influence transmuted into family wealth. In traditional times the Chinese gentry advanced itself by dispatching one son to run the family farm, another to operate the family business, and a third to seek high office, with the understanding that each would help to expand their common patrimony where he could. In the modern-day version of this strategy, the father holds high office while his offspring seek out commercial opportunities which he quietly protects and promotes.

Even the rural enterprises that have driven so much of China's economic growth over the past twenty years are controlled by local Communist Party secretaries and their kinsmen, not by Bill Gates–type entrepreneurs. China does not just suffer from crony capitalism, but from a full-blown case of communist kleptocracy. A large part of China's much-vaunted "private sector" remains, directly or indirectly, under the control of Party bosses. Many of China's new class of capitalists are consanguineous to the old Party elite. In this sense, China's economic reform has been hijacked by the current power holders, who are unremittingly hostile to free-market democracy.

Myth:
THE PULL OF AMERICAN CULTURE WILL MAKE CHINA INTO THE MIRROR IMAGE OF THE UNITED STATES

While the materialistic aspects of American culture, Hollywood style, are attractive to the Chinese, they find other aspects—namely its rampant hedonism, sex and violence—unappealing and even repulsive. The spread of American pop culture to China is not a sign of political convergence. As Samuel Huntington has perceptively remarked, the Big Mac is not the Magna Carta.

Most of the tens of thousands of Chinese students who come to the United States remain here, and thus can hardly serve as agents of change in their homeland. Taiwan's President Lee Teng-hui holds a Ph.D. from Cornell University, but there is not a single minister of anything in the People's Republic who has an American university degree. Those who do return home with advanced degrees in, say, nuclear engineering bring with them technical expertise but little commitment to democratic change. China's military-industrial complex may contain U.S.-trained scientists drinking Coke, smoking Marlboros and eating Kentucky Fried Chicken, but when they go to work they stay busy making mini–nuclear warheads based on stolen U.S. plans to aim at American cities.

Westerners, whose belief in "progress" predisposes them to a linear view of history, imagine that each new generation of Chinese will be more Western-oriented and democratically-minded than the last. But the Chinese view of history is cyclical, not linear. Despite a quarter-century of exposure to the West, the Chinese who grew up under Mao have not lost their distinctive attitudes toward society, government and culture, which are fundamentally utilitarian. It was not idealism but utilitarianism that led Chinese youth to admire the U.S. in the eighties, just as it was not ideology but utilitarianism that has led them to give tacit support to authoritarian rule in the new millennium.

When Deng Xiaoping opened the door to the West, there loomed America, the wealthiest and most advanced country the world had ever known. The Chinese were instantly infatuated with the democratic superpower. Many of them eagerly embraced the free market and the open political system which they judged, rightly, to be the twin sources of America's strength. Throughout the eighties rapid improvements in living standards seemed to confirm their choice of this new paradigm. The students who participated in the 1989 demonstrations were impatient to move even faster in the direction they were convinced would lift China up to superpower status. By emulating even more closely their chosen model, the United States, they hoped not only to open their society but also to restore China to its paramount place among nations.

It was not the Tiananmen massacre alone that shattered this hope, but the economic debacle and political chaos in Russia and the former Soviet republics. The Beijing regime has encouraged the view that Western-style democracy destroyed the economies of the former Soviet Union and Eastern Europe, sending them deep into recession, and has been at pains to point out that China has taken a different path. In the words of Wang Zhenyao, a Ministry of Civil Affairs official who has spent the last dozen years supervising elections in China's villages, "In the Soviet Union, they just pulled down the Communist Party, and leapt straight into privatization. Elite change was far ahead of grassroots change."[8]

China's booming economy, achieved under a heavy-handed but stable authoritarian regime, has convinced many that the regime is right. Authoritarian rule, they believe, is necessary for China to enjoy the stability it needs to develop economically and catch up to the West.

Myth:
THE COMMUNICATIONS REVOLUTION
AND THE INTERNET WILL CHANGE CHINA

The Chinese invented paper, so it is fitting that China is once again one of the great writing and publishing nations on the planet. The contrast with the heyday of Mao Zedong, when all the foolscap in China was reserved for printing tens of millions of copies of *The Little Red Book*, could not be starker. Now, literally thousands of titles are published each year, along with hundreds of periodicals, newspapers, and other publications.

Western visitors to China assume that this massive outpouring of print contains a wide variety of political opinions. But what in fact are Chinese writers writing, and readers reading? This is a hard question to answer because very little of this huge outpouring of prose is finding its way into translation, and China's idiographic script is notoriously difficult to learn. That which is published in English loses much of its depth and resonance, or leaves Western readers groping for meaning. What does it mean to read that Mao was more ruthless than the First Emperor of the Qin dynasty, or that his wife, Jiang Qing, was more of a schemer than Empress Wu of the Han? Every language draws a magic circle of meaning around the culture it defines and expresses, noted the linguist

Edward Sapir. Around Chinese there is not merely a circle but a semantic Great Wall built of obscure historical allusions, hoary cultural practices, and veiled political references.

As the Sinologist Geremie Barme has recently argued, "After the death of Mao Zedong and the gradual ideological demobilization of the country, the arts came increasingly under the sway of a new-style leader, the party technocrat."[9] Artistic expression is allowed, but only within widely recognized political boundary markers. Criticism of the Chinese Communist Party, its chief instruments of control (the People's Liberation Army, the Ministry of State Security), and its principal policies (the one-child-per-family rule, etc.) is beyond the pale. Promoting radical nationalism is acceptable, advocating Western-style democracy is not.[10]

Self-censorship by writers greatly eases the state's burden of enforcing cultural orthodoxy. Shen Hao, editor of a tabloid called the *Southern Weekend*, tries to print "real news," but admits, "There's always a sense of pressure and a feeling that you can't be completely independent."[11] The government has and will shut down privately owned publishing houses if they trespass into forbidden realms, and ban individual books and magazines. In practice, however, this is seldom necessary. The vast majority of Chinese writers exercise their refined artistic sensibilities not only in their work, but also in keeping their work—and themselves—out of political trouble, if not always in the good graces of officialdom. Thus, the relationship between state and writer today is not adversarial but collaborative, almost symbiotic.

The writing that emerges from this melding of the artistic and the official mind is much more sophisticated than the socialist realist kitsch that formerly characterized Chinese literature, but is still cast in an officially approved mold. Nihilism is discouraged but individualism is allowed, particularly when it fosters materialistic or entrepreneurial sentiments. The enormously popular *Houhei* ("thick and black") movement, for example, has spawned a whole genre of literature based on the writings of a Chinese Machiavelli, Li Zongwu, who explains in *The Science of the Thick and the Black* that "We all are born with a face, and to be thick-skinned is its prerogative. God also gives us a heart, and it can be as black as pitch. . . . All things dear to man can come from being thick-skinned and black-hearted: fame and wealth, palaces, wives, concubines, clothes, chariots, and horses." Not only did the book sell many hundreds of thousands of copies but its leading publisher was none other than the Central Party School, the training ground for China's political commissars.

But China change theorists look less to books than to the proliferation of information-exchange technologies made possible by trade and economic reform, such as e-mail, faxes, and cellular telephones, which they expect to create an irresistible momentum toward openness. In this view, the Internet turns every computer screen into a window on the wider world and unlocks every cerebral door. In fact, however, the Chinese leadership has seen the dangers of the communications revolution, and is aggressively moving to meet it. It is, to be sure, almost impossible to monitor e-mail or stop it from getting through. But the China Democracy Party has reported that its Web site and other pro-democracy on-line publications have been wiped out by destructive computer viruses engineered by China's police. Chinese who promote such Web sites have been prosecuted for "inciting the overthrow of state power." Cyber-reporters have been banned.[12]

But Beijing is not content merely to restrict access to the Internet. It is building a Great Wall in cyberspace—an *Intra*net that will function as a high-tech Potemkin Village from which all uncensored foreign news, including financial news, will be excluded. Millions of Chinese users will soon be logging onto this Intranet thinking that it will give them unrestricted access to information from around the world. They will actually be entering an antiseptic environment which has been carefully swept for all "dangerous" content. A great deal of costly advanced technology will be required to set up a Chinese Intranet, but it is part of a grand strategy for controlling information that may even involve public security officials setting up a few subversive-looking sites as a way of entrapping unwary critics of the regime.

For Lao Zi also said, "The Sage rules thus: he empties their minds, stuffs their bellies, weakens their will, and strengthens their bodies. He always keeps the people devoid of intelligence and desire. He keeps the intelligent in fear from action, and all are governed." *(Lao Zi, ch. 3)*

Myth:
OUR OWN FEARS BLIND US TO THE FACT
THAT CHINA HAS ALREADY CHANGED

The boldest of China's defenders put the "China threat" in quotes and suggest that it is a figment of the paranoid American imagination. James Schlesinger, energy secretary under President Carter and later a China trader, advises us that "America should relax about China and resist the Cold War reflex, with every Chinese advance, to grab a shovel to dig that bomb shelter in the backyard."[13] We should work to overcome our feelings that China is a rogue state to be contained, these analysts tell us, and come to see it as a responsible power to be embraced.

But it was Paramount Leader Deng Xiaoping himself who in September 1991 first characterized the conflict between the U.S. and China as "a new cold war."[14] Such warlike words are regularly repeated in the Chinese press and in the speeches of senior leaders. "Western hostile forces," declared President Jiang Zemin in August 1995, "have not for a moment abandoned their plot to Westernize and 'divide' our country."[15] The Chinese state has targeted the U.S. with ICBMs, and publicly declares that we are its "enemy." Underlying such rhetoric and actions are real and continuing differences between our two countries. According to a confidential Chinese military document, "Because China and the United States have long-standing conflicts over their different ideologies, social systems, and foreign policies, it will prove impossible to fundamentally improve Sino-U.S. relations."[16]

The continuing bluster of China's leaders is not some Cold War fantasy generated by American nativism, but a clear expression of their hegemonic desire to become, once again, the largest, most powerful civilization on earth. As Arthur Waldron has remarked, "China remains a self-perpetuating communist dictatorship, a regime for which lawless coercion remains very much a fundamental tool of politics—not only domestically, but in foreign policy as well. Therefore China almost by definition poses a potential threat to her neighbors and to the U.S."[17]

The American-dominated global system is most effective in defusing conflict in those regions of the world where American primacy is unchallenged, among nations with compatible sociopolitical systems. With China's political elite ruling by force of arms, and already challenging American leadership in East Asia, it would be naive to expect a multilateral framework dominated by the U.S. to be capable of checking China's ambitions in the absence of fundamental changes in the way that country is governed. It is one thing to convince a third-rate dictator of a banana republic that it is in his interest to consent to the American way of doing things; it is quite another to convince the political and military elite of the Middle Kingdom—Legalist heirs of a two-thousand-year tradition of supremacy in Asia—to relinquish power at home voluntarily and consent to permanent American global superiority. The present rulers of China will never consent to Taiwan as a permanent vassal state of the United States, nor willingly retreat from the South China Sea. And once these territories are reunited with the motherland, China's rulers will seek to extend their sphere of influence further afield. As George Melloan has recently written, "China's unspoken goal is to destroy America's power."[18]

CLINTON'S "STRATEGIC PARTNERSHIP"

If any of these myths were true, American ways would effortlessly come to dominate in China. Democratic sentiments would grow apace with the growing Chinese middle class. Chinese youth (dressed in Levis) would meet (at McDonald's) to discuss human rights. Internet chat rooms would be devoted to setting up opposition political parties. E-mails and faxes would encourage people to turn out for political rallies. Before we knew it, China would be abiding by the rule of law, enacting a written constitution, and holding free elections. The Goddess of Democracy would make a return to her throne in Tiananmen Square. China would follow

America's lead in the Asia-Pacific Economic Cooperation Forum (APEC) and cooperate with the American-dominated World Bank and International Monetary Fund. Beijing would recognize Taiwan as a separate and equal state, and give up its smash-and-grab operations in the South China Sea. The United States would enjoy a true "strategic partnership" with China.

Elements of all these myths of China's liberalization came to characterize the China policy of the Clinton administration's last years. Before he was elected, Bill Clinton regularly excoriated George Bush for "coddling tyrants from Baghdad to Beijing," and promised to get tough with China on human rights. But once he was president, Clinton bowed to Chinese threats and reversed himself, extending Most Favored Nation status to that country despite its abysmal record on human rights. "I hate our China policy!" Clinton reportedly screamed at his advisors following his humiliating capitulation. "I wish I was running against our China policy. I mean, we gave them MFN and we change our commercial policy, and what has it changed?"[19]

In 1996, when the PLA began lobbing M-9 nuclear-capable ballistic missiles into the waters off Taiwan, Clinton reversed himself again, sending two carrier battle groups to the area in a public show of force, and warning Beijing privately of "grave consequences" if it continued its warlike acts. Consequently, Beijing retreated. The obvious lesson of the incident—that peace had been maintained across the Taiwan Strait through a show of strength— was unfortunately lost on a nervous White House. No sooner had Clinton made his great display of force than he determined to reverse course once more. He opened a "second channel" to China through National Security Advisor Sandy Berger, bypassing Secretary of State Warren Christopher, and attempted to mollify Beijing's fierce wrath on the issue of Taiwan, and by extension other contentious issues in U.S.-China relations, through a policy of dialogue, accommodation, and ultimately, appeasement.

By 1998, the Clinton administration's flip-flop came to rest. The U.S. and China, we now learned, were "strategic partners." To cement this new relationship, Clinton announced that he would personally go to China and meet with Communist leader Jiang Zemin.

Well before President Clinton and his entourage of 1,200 landed in China on June 25,1998, the Chinese authorities were making extensive preparations for his visit. Chinese cities were spruced up, Clinton was given a new and more favorable image in the Chinese press, publications were told to toe the party line, meetings with carefully selected "ordinary" citizens were arranged, and democracy advocates were either arrested or warned not to do anything that would spoil the first visit of an American president since George Bush went to China in 1989. Leaders of house churches and the underground Catholic Church were warned to keep a low profile, and Catholic Bishop Julias Jia Zhiguo, whose diocese is in northern Hebei province near Beijing, was preemptively arrested.[20] Three democracy campaigners from Hangzhou who braved the repression by attempting to register a new political party, the Chinese Democracy Party, were quickly taken into custody.[21]

Clinton arrived at his first stop in Xian to find that the city's leading democracy advocates had been detained or sent into temporary exile the day before. How many dissidents were hustled out of sight is not known, but enough reports reached the American press for the *New York Times* to call the arrests a "serious embarrass[ment]" for the president, to which he must "respond personally, publicly, and bluntly."[22] Yet the normally loquacious Clinton had little to say. The detentions were "disturbing," he remarked mildly, but such behavior "makes it all the more important that we continue to work with the Chinese and engage them."

Unlike President Reagan, who in 1988 had met with a hundred Soviet dissidents at the American embassy in Moscow, or President Bush, who in 1989 had invited China's leading dissident, Fang Lizhi, to a state dinner, Clinton had no plans to meet with dissidents.[23] Quietly pressing Jiang to release whole groups of political prisoners, his aides assured reporters privately, would be more effective than "theatrical" encounters with dissidents. No such amnesties were declared by the Chinese, then or later.

The only hint of a rebuke in Clinton's brief remarks at the

welcoming ceremony in Xian was directed not at Beijing, but at his own domestic critics "who wonder whether closer ties and deeper friendship between America and China are good." His answer was unequivocal: "Clearly, the answer is yes."

The summit meeting between President Clinton and Chinese President Jiang Zemin took place two days later in Beijing, after a controversial welcoming ceremony on Tiananmen Square that seemed to rub U.S. policy makers' noses in the history of the past decade. The two presidents met for ninety minutes, approving a series of agreements, most of them minor, that had been negotiated in advance. These included a joint commitment not to provide assistance to ballistic missile programs in South Asia, an agreement "on the importance" of China's long-pending entry into the World Trade Organization, and a promise that China would "actively study" joining the missile technology control regime.

The most widely trumpeted agreement involved a pledge by both sides not to target their ballistic missiles at each other. This meant little in military terms, both because it was not subject to verification and because the missiles can be retargeted in a matter of minutes. (Retargeting is actually the least time-consuming of China's war preparations, since China's strategic rockets are stored without their liquid fuel or their warheads.) Nor was it a priority for the Chinese side. For the Clinton administration, involved in an ongoing controversy over the possible transfer of missile technology to China by Loral and Hughes, the agreement was an important way of defusing domestic criticism.

Another concession to Clinton was Jiang's last-minute decision to carry the seventy-minute press conference that followed live on nationwide Chinese television, though without the prior announcement that would have guaranteed a large audience. This allowed Clinton to speak directly to the Chinese people on such questions as personal freedom, the nature of democratic government, Tiananmen Square, and the Dalai Lama.

The president did not exactly run with the ball. In his comments on human rights, for example, Clinton said, "We Americans firmly believe that individual rights, including the freedom of speech, association and religion, are very important not only to those who exercise them, but also to nations, whose success in the 21st century depends upon widespread individual knowledge, creativity, free exchange and enterprise." Rather than insisting that there are fundamental, God-given freedoms which no government has the right to suppress, Clinton used the utilitarian argument that freedom is necessary for economic success.

On the issue of Tiananmen, Clinton told Jiang that the use of force to end peaceful demonstrations was "wrong," but this seeming rebuke was delivered in vague, relativistic terms that blunted its force. "[N]ine years ago, Chinese citizens of all ages raised their voices for democracy," Clinton began. "For all of our agreements, we still disagree about the meaning of what happened then. I believe and the American people believe that the use of force and the tragic loss of life was wrong." In fact there was little ambiguity about the meaning of Tiananmen, and Clinton's phrase "tragic loss of life" made "what happened then" sound more like a plane crash than the willful massacre of several thousand people.[24]

What did Jiang get in return for the missile targeting agreement, his denial that his agents had illegally contributed to Clinton's party coffers, and the "Clinton Live" broadcast replete with the president's guilty efforts to propose a theory of moral equivalence? His broad objective in hosting a "summit meeting" with the American president was international recognition of China's growing importance. More particularly, he was looking for a final rehabilitation of his government in the eyes of the world a decade after Tiananmen, a gesture that would close the books on the massacre and consolidate his own power at home. Other Western leaders had traveled to Beijing in the years since unarmed demonstrators were shot down in the streets of China's capital city, but Bill Clinton was the first American president to do so. The image of the leader of the free world toeing the line on Tiananmen, the Beijing regime hoped, would exorcise the ghosts of the pro-democracy martyrs forever.

The chief concession that Clinton made to produce "strategic partnership" involved democratic Taiwan. At a meeting with intellectuals in Shanghai, Clinton responded to a planted question by mouthing Beijing's "three no's" formula: "We don't support independence for Taiwan; or two Chinas; or one Taiwan, one China. And we don't believe that Taiwan should be a member in any organization for which statehood is a requirement." With these words Clinton became the first American president to side with China's dictators and publicly oppose self-determination for the twenty-one million people of Taiwan.

Clinton explained that "Our country recognized China and *embraced* a 'one-China' policy almost twenty years ago." Not exactly. While the U.S. extended diplomatic recognition to the PRC as the sole legitimate government of China in 1979, it merely *"acknowledged* the Chinese position that there is but one China and Taiwan is part of China" (italics added). This careful ambiguity left open the possibility that China's claim might one day no longer be true—a possibility now foreclosed by Clinton.[25]

Following this kowtow, a host of Clinton administration officials, led by Secretary of State Madeleine Albright, were quick to suggest that the president was only stating what had long been implicit in U.S. policy. Nothing has changed, insisted White House spokesman Mike McCurry. But Clinton's new tilt toward China was certainly obvious enough to Taipei and Beijing. "The United States and the Chinese Communists have no right and are in no position to conduct bilateral negotiations on anything related to our affairs," declared Taiwan government spokesman Roy Wu. "It's wrong, morally and politically, for Clinton to collude with the Communist dictatorship to restrict the future of a democratic country, Taiwan," insisted Parris Chang, a leader of the pro-independence Democratic Progressive Party.

Only two years before, the presence of U.S. aircraft carriers off Taiwan had sent an unmistakable signal that the U.S. would not stand idly by while China tried to reunify Taiwan by force. Now Clinton sent a very different message by reciting China's "three no's," creating the impression that the U.S. was strong-arming Taiwan to the negotiating table and might even stand aside if China invaded, especially if this event were to follow a Taiwanese declaration of independence.

China's ambitions are not limited to Taiwan, of course. Beijing would like to see the U.S. disengage from Asia as a whole, particularly from its military alliance with Japan, so that it would be free to bring the region within its own sphere of influence. The Chinese sought to underline symbolically their growing importance in Asia—and to distance the U.S. from its long-term allies in the region—by insisting that the president not stop in any other Asian country during that trip. The White House agreed, and Clinton broke precedent by not stopping over in Japan en route to or from China in order to brief Japanese leaders on the summit. The short visit by Secretary of State Albright to Tokyo after the China trip only served to underscore the president's absence.

As China well knows, demanding that the U.S.-China relationship come first necessarily requires that the U.S. put its allies second. Clinton seems to have adopted this approach after arriving in China, to judge from the pointed criticisms of Japanese economic policy that he, along with Treasury Secretary Robert Rubin and other administration officials, issued in the course of their economic dialogue with China during the nine-day visit. At the joint press conference in Beijing, for example, Clinton responded to a question on the falling Japanese yen by making Japan sound like a wayward pupil of American *and* China: "President Jiang and I would give anything to be able to just wave a wand and have all of [Japan's economic problems] go away. We are not the only actors in this drama, and a lot of this must be done by the Japanese government and the Japanese people. We can be supportive, but they have to make the right decision." After arriving in Shanghai, which he gushingly characterized as "one of the very most exciting places in the entire world," the president called again for Japan to do more about the Asian financial crisis. The leaders of the world's second-largest economy, which has been a reliable ally of the United States for more than a half-century, must have been wondering what they had done to deserve such rebukes directed at them from Chinese soil by an American president.[26]

Clinton was upbeat at his final press conference in Hong Kong, especially where Jiang Zemin was concerned. He surprised reporters by calling Jiang, hitherto viewed as a rather colorless Communist Party boss, a leader of "vision" who was "clearly committed to reform." Answering a question about China's democratic prospects, he went even further: Not only would China evolve into a pluralistic democracy, Clinton predicted, but it would be President Jiang himself who would dismantle the existing one-party dictatorship and lead China into the twenty-first century.

Clinton's visit to China was compared to President Richard Nixon's 1972 trip. Yet while Nixon's China gambit against an aggressive and hostile Soviet Union played to bipartisan support and a universally admiring press, Clinton's proposed "strategic partnership" with China was difficult for him and his aides to define. Asked how it can be in America's national interest to tilt Asia's balance of power away from long-time, democratic allies like Japan, Korea, and Taiwan in favor of a regime implacably hostile to American values, his aides simply retreated into silence. Asked what countries the U.S. and China were "strategizing" against, his aides explained that the new partnership was not a military alliance. But no one in the administration apparently bothered to check their Chinese and Japanese dictionaries before settling upon the word "strategic." In both languages this word has strongly militaristic overtones. Indeed, it contains the very character for "war" (zhan in Chinese, sen in Japanese). To the amusement of the Chinese, then, and to the horror of the Japanese, Clinton appeared to be suggesting a U.S.-China military alliance. The administration, which had not seriously considered the implications of this phrase when applied to China, later dropped it in favor of "engagement" when questions arose.

Yet thought its behavior was clumsy and its politics often inchoate, the Clinton administration was not alone in searching for a post–Cold War, post-Tiananmen justification for maintaining close ties to the Beijing regime. In the aftermath of Tiananmen, with U.S.-China relations strained to the breaking point, Henry Kissinger suggested that the U.S. needed China as a counterweight not merely to the Soviet Union but also to Japan. At a press conference several months later, former President Bush seemed to lend credence to the notion of a "Japan threat." The idea that America would side with a nuclear-armed communist regime against a non-nuclear democracy that it was obligated by treaty to defend from attack was quickly disavowed by embarrassed officials.[27]

Zbigniew Brzezinski, President Jimmy Carter's National Security Advisor, is among those who argue for continued strategic cooperation between the U.S. and China. Brzezinski argues that the U.S. needs an ally to hold down the eastern end of the Eurasian mainland—a Far Eastern Anchor, he calls it—and that China is the natural choice to fill such a role. Japan, however important in other respects, is disqualified by virtue of being an offshore island chain. In Brzezinski's own words, "A close relationship with maritime Japan is essential for America's global policy, but a cooperative relationship with mainland China is imperative for America's Eurasian geostrategy."[28] Translated into plain English, what Brzezinski is saying is that America still needs China to keep Russia in check.

It takes a great deal of imagination to see Russia as a threat at a time when all indicators of national strength and well-being, from GDP to average lifespan, are in precipitous decline. Brzezinski recognizes that the disintegration of the "world's territorially largest state created a 'black hole' in the very center of Eurasia," yet at the same time he remains preoccupied by the possibility of a resurgent Russian Empire. To forestall this possibility, he suggests "a loosely confederated Russia . . . less susceptible to imperial mobilization . . . composed of a European Russia, a Siberian Republic, and a Far Eastern Republic," a tripartite division hauntingly reminiscent of the historical division and ultimate extinction of Poland by its three more powerful neighbors, one of which was of course Russia. One suspects that China would applaud such decentralization, since the Russian Far East corresponds so neatly to the territory that Russia wrenched away from China a century ago. The complete political separation of the Russian Far East and Siberia from the European Russian homeland would deliver both into the hands of China.

Brzezinski does indicate that he sees the handwriting on the Great Wall when he acknowledges that "A 'Greater China' may be emerging, whatever the desires and calculations of its neighbors"; but then he goes on to caution that "any effort to prevent that from happening could entail an intensifying conflict with China" which would "strain American-Japanese relations." His advice is not just that we do nothing, but even worse, that we actively collude with China to create a sphere of influence that will satisfy it. "[A]ccommodation with China will . . . exact its own price," writes Brzezinski. "To accept China as a regional power is not a matter of simply endorsing a mere slogan. There will have to be substance to any such regional preeminence. To put it very directly, how large a Chinese sphere of influence, and where, should America be prepared to accept as part of a policy of successfully co-opting China into world affairs? What areas now outside of China's political radius might have to be conceded to the realm of the reemerging Celestial Empire?"[29]

This kind of accommodation could easily drift into appeasement, where the only issues under discussion are the precise timing of the American retreat and the names of the U.S. allies to be left to China's tender mercies. For if the principal goal of U.S. foreign policy becomes the avoidance of conflict with China in Asia for the sake of integrating it into a global condominium, then America must give way to China's regional ambitions. Which democratic states will we watch being devoured by the Hegemon? Taiwan? Kazakhstan? Mongolia? Thailand? Brzezinski and all those in the foreign policy establishment who think as he does are silent on this point.

CHAPTER SEVEN

Containing the Hegemon

T he beginnings of the current U.S. policy towards China are to be found in Henry Kissinger's secretive first mission to Beijing when, as Nixon's national security advisor, he flatly pledged to Zhou Enlai—*without extracting any concessions in return*—that the U.S. would oppose an independent Taiwan. So eager was Kissinger to be able to play the China card against the Soviet threat that he also tried to minimize the deep ideological divide between China and the U.S. The Clinton administration's "strategic partnership" is a direct descendant of Kissinger's promiscuous embrace of Zhou Enlai, and is based on making preemptive concessions on a wide range of trade and security issues in return for nothing more tangible than the hope that China will be nice. To name this policy for what it is—appeasement—is to recognize it as a failure. Shorn of its strategic rationale by the collapse of the Soviet Union and stripped of its ideological blinders by the Tiananmen massacre, it is also an embarrassment.

Acting on the assumption that China responds best to incentives, the Clinton administration repeatedly made gifts of supercomputers, satellites, and other technology to the Beijing regime, expecting in return that China would respond to its entreaties to stop peddling nuclear, chemical and perhaps biological weapons and the missiles to deliver them. But contrary to its promises, China has continued trafficking in nuclear-weapons-related materials with Iran, just as it earlier armed Pakistan with enough fissionable material to make several nuclear weapons, and sent ballistic missile technology to North Korea, Saudi Arabia and Libya.[1]

The Clinton administration argued that its policy of "engagement" had fostered stability in Asia. But it was on Clinton's watch that China seized islands in the South China Sea, fired missiles in the direction of Taiwan, and continued to increase its military spending at a double-digit pace. The Chinese government even tried to subvert American elections in 1996. But the Clinton-Jiang summit proceeded nonetheless. Even after revelations about Chinese spies in American nuclear facilities, the Clinton administration continued to approve the sale of militarily useful equipment, such as the special explosive bolts used in separating the different stages of a missile, and state-of-the-art supercomputers.[2]

Acting on the assumption that, on the human rights front, China responded better to "quiet diplomacy" than to public criticism, the Clinton administration delinked human rights and trade, backed away from economic sanctions, and began quietly peddling excuses for China's behavior. In response, Beijing released a couple of well-known dissidents, then quietly carried out a nationwide crackdown that has left most of the country's other dissidents either in jail or under house arrest. The China Democracy Party founders are serving long prison sentences. Arrests of Christian leaders continue. Even the leaders of the nonpolitical Falun Gong, a Buddhist exercise group, now find themselves in jail. Their crime: asking to be legally recognized as an "association."

Nor has the Clinton administration's "engagement" kept China from engaging in such inhumane practices as forced abortion and religious repression, or inventing new horrors like selling prisoners' organs and lethal injection of "illegal" babies at birth. Clinton has averted his gaze, while his spokesmen have made sympathetic noises about China's population problem and the dangers of uncontrolled religious activity. "The Administration has always argued that its policy of engagement will make China more like us," Robert Kagan and William Kristol have perceptively remarked. "In fact, it is making us more like them."[3]

After two full decades of economic reform, the Chinese Communist Party on August 9, 1999, asked its members to study a new book entitled *Marx, Engels, Lenin, Stalin, Mao Zedong, Deng*

Xiaoping and Jiang Zemin Discuss Materialism and Atheism.[4] This does not suggest a regime that is becoming more tolerant of differing religious and cultural views. Nor is the regime's commitment to maintaining a "socialist market economy," with substantial control over important economic sectors, noticeably on the wane. Fully confident that their view of economics will ultimately prevail, leading Chinese strategists assert that in years to come it is not China but the United States that will change, in a "transition away from capitalism . . . toward some type of 'socialist market economy.'"[5]

The same China that, driven by its history and its cultural hubris, regards the U.S. with hostility today will likely be taking an even more critical view of American power in the Pacific twenty years from now. China's unspoken goal then, as now, will be to destroy that power. China's ambitions to establish a *Pax Sinica*, which predate the founding of the U.S. by a couple of millennia, will remain in place. The only thing that will have changed is China's military capabilities, which will have expanded greatly.

How to deal with the Hegemon? The first step is to take a page out of the Cold War playbook and begin thinking in terms of containment. If successful, containment by the United States would prevent China from gaining effective sway over its immediate neighbors, limit its influence further afield, and thwart the emergence of a Eurasian superpower that would threaten America's global interests. It would require, first, acknowledging the realities of Chinese aims, and then constraining the modernization of military technology, keeping China in such a clear position of military inferiority that Beijing would avoid at all costs a direct military collision. The deployment of a missile defense system at the same time would avert China's use of nuclear blackmail against America and its allies. Meanwhile, a variety of measures could promote a peaceful political evolution that would gradually break down China's closed system and replace it with an open, democratic one. In buying time for China's dissidents and democrats, on the mainland, in Hong Kong, and on Taiwan, we buy time for ourselves.

What, specifically, should we do to domesticate the Hegemon?

NO MORE MAOTAIS

The perpetuation of the failed Nixon-Kissinger policy has to do not only with Chinese pressure and simple bureaucratic inertia, but also with the self-interest of those carrying it out. It is a scandal that most former secretaries of state (beginning with Henry Kissinger), most former national security advisors (also beginning with Kissinger) and most of their senior deputies have gone into the China trade subsequent to their government service, often without even allowing the passage of a decent interval before beginning to cash in. Richard Holbrooke, President Carter's assistant secretary of state for East Asia and Pacific Affairs, for example, was in Beijing within a few months of leaving his administration post, by which time he had become a consultant for Lehman Brothers and an adviser to Nike and Seagram. Alexander Haig, President Reagan's first secretary of state, went to work for United Technologies after leaving office in June 1982, where he continued as an advocate of selling arms to China.[6]

Such profiteering, either past or anticipated, cannot help but color the views of those who would engage in it, generating a peace-at-any-price attitude toward U.S.-China relations, and color too the advice they give the nation in their capacity as "experts." Understanding this, Beijing holds them hostage to their avarice and summons them into action whenever some irritant in U.S.-China relations arises. They are quick to apologize for Beijing when it commits some outrageous act, such as gunning down unarmed demonstrators in the heart of the capital city. What else could account for Kissinger's cold-blooded assertion, just weeks after the Tiananmen massacre, that "No government in the world would have tolerated having the main square of its capital occupied for eight weeks by tens of thousands of demonstrators who blocked the area in front of the main government buildings"?[7]

TECHNOLOGY TRANSFER

During the Cold War there were strict controls on the export of dual-use technology—technology that has military as well as commercial applications—by the U.S. and its allies to prevent dangerous technology from falling into the hands of potential adversaries. Under the Clinton administration these controls were largely dismantled, and some of our best technology, sometimes in defiance of the recommendations of experts, has been approved for sale to China. "On at least two occasions," Michael Ledeen has written, "military experts who argued against high-tech exports to China later discovered that their recommendations had been altered in the Pentagon's computerized data base."[8] Other experts have been silenced or coerced into lying.

The U.S. should tighten up its technology transfer policy towards China and restore strict controls over dual-use exports. The export of advanced telecommunications equipment and supercomputers should be carefully reviewed. Stiff penalties should be imposed on firms whose negligence compromises U.S. security. Chinese requests for the transfer of technology should be reviewed by a multilateral committee comparable to that which governed exports to the former Soviet Union, and denied where they compromise U.S. security in some way.

MISSILE DEFENSES

Whatever future controls are placed on technology transfers will not affect the missile technology that China has already purchased from Russia or stolen from the U.S. To defend against China's rapidly growing arsenal of ballistic missiles, the U.S. should deploy first an Asian and then a national missile-defense system. The protective umbrella of the Asian regional missile-defense system should extend over Japan, Korea, and other U.S. allies in the region including Taiwan. Guarding the Taiwanese from ballistic-missile attack by China is especially critical given the rapid and ongoing build-up of medium-range ballistic missiles along the Fujian coast opposite Taiwan. The sale of the requested four Aegis-class antimissile ships to Taiwan would be another step in the right direction.

In August 1999, China test-fired its first DF-31, a long-range ballistic missile capable of hitting the western United States. A national missile defense system capable of defending U.S. cities against this new generation of Chinese missiles must be built and deployed as soon as technologically feasible. Once such a system is in place, China will not be able to blackmail the United States with nuclear weapons.

"IMPERIAL OVERSTRETCH" REVERSED

Chinese strategists believe as an article of faith that the U.S. is a power in decline, that it will eventually withdraw from Asia and abandon its bases in the region. They also believe that, without these forward bases, America's fundamental logistics weaknesses will be revealed, namely, that it "must cross the Atlantic or Pacific Oceans and go to Europe or Asia" to engage in combat, and that it lacks sufficient transport capacity to do so. Maintaining a strong, forward-deployed military presence in Asia will expose these beliefs as misperceptions, and thus help the Chinese leadership to avoid the strategic miscalculations that are so often the cause of out-and-out military conflict.[9]

The best antidote to these dangerous misperceptions about American capabilities is a carefully calculated build-up of naval and air force elements in Asia. President Ronald Reagan met the challenge of Soviet power directly through an arms build-up and a policy of confronting Soviet aggression wherever it occurred. History has demonstrated the success of this policy, which should be adopted in Asia. An air wing or two deployed in hardened bunkers, or a second carrier task force on patrol in the region, or both, would force the Chinese elite to rethink their facile (and factually wrong) assumptions about declining U.S. military power. Some increase in our air and sea-lift capacity is also called for, so that additional assets could be quickly deployed to the Asian theater in the event of hostilities. By challenging China's misperceptions, and by meeting its growing power projection capabilities head-on, we would underscore for Beijing the cost of competing with the U.S.

Some argue that China will become a military superpower regardless of what the U.S. does—or doesn't do—to try to forestall it. In their view, a strategic stalemate with the United States is the most likely outcome of China's resurgence. But this isn't a preordained outcome. After all, while Russia still has most of its nuclear arsenal, it is no longer generally considered a superpower because of the economic collapse and the decline of its conventional forces that resulted from U.S. containment. And there is nothing inevitable about China's economic growth. Mismanagement could drive the economy into a recession or worse. So could increased defense spending. This is a reason for upping the ante to the point where China is unable to compete with the U.S. militarily except by taking scarce resources away from vital infrastructure projects and economic development in general. Forced to confront this stark choice, the Chinese Politburo may well choose plowshares over swords. (The collapse of the Soviet Union is widely understood in China to be a consequence of its extraordinarily high defense spending.) But even if the Politburo makes the "wrong" decision and attempts to keep pace with the U.S., it would so hamstring its economic and technological development that, in the end, it would be unable to compete.

The People's Liberation Army generals were initially stunned by the American victory in the Gulf War. In the mocking words of one Chinese analyst, "People turned pale at the mere mention of U.S. military strength." But the years since, in a peculiar turnabout, have seen a concerted effort by Chinese analysts to minimize America's strengths and elaborate on American "weaknesses." We are said to have been "defeated" in Vietnam and Korea, and to have played only a secondary role in winning World War II. (In this revisionist view, Russia and China were the principal victors.) Our military capabilities are said to be in decline, and we have only a "30 percent chance" of winning a war in Asia. Chinese strategists apparently believe, according to Michael Pillsbury, that "Saddam Hussein could have exploited [U.S. operational weaknesses] in order to defeat the United States [in the Gulf War] if he had used Chinese-style strategy."[10]

A modest build-up of U.S. assets in Asia would force the Chinese elite to take a fresh look at U.S. power and potential. Our goal would be to convince them that facile predictions of the decline of what Ben Wattenberg calls "the first universal nation" are premature. The halcyon days of U.S.-China relations, it is well to remember, occurred during the years of the Reagan administration, when China quailed before the U.S. military build-up and put on its most cooperative face, taking the advice of Sun-tzu: When outnumbered, retreat.

SITUATIONS OF STRENGTH

Like any other maritime state, the U.S. needs to control not only its own shores but also the waters beyond, and it particularly needs to have friends, allies, and bases on or near opposite shores. We cannot entrust our security to an uncritical "engagement" with China based on the assumption that Beijing will allow itself to be placated. The continuation, or restoration, of our alliances with Japan, Korea, Taiwan, and the Philippines is essential as China's power grows. As a distant maritime superpower, the U.S. can offer the littoral states security against Chinese encroachments without arousing fears that it harbors territorial ambitions of its own. This security umbrella is particularly important vis-à-vis Japan, for in the absence of a strong U.S. presence in Asia, Japan would either be forced to rearm or would be drawn willy-nilly into China's orbit.

Our overall goal should be to create, in Dean Acheson's phrase, "situations of strength" at every point of the compass where the PRC may be tempted to break out. We should aim to strengthen our ties with our Asian-Pacific allies, and look beyond this to possible accommodations with Russia, India, and Indonesia. If our ties with our allies are sound, we can keep the peace even if China remains a threat.[11]

The U.S.-Japan link is the linchpin of U.S. treaty commitments in Asia. The four decades of the Cold War proved that Japan could be the largest—and most stable—platform for U.S. power projection in Northeast Asia, for securing both shores of the Pacific as well as facilitating U.S. operations into Southeast Asia and beyond. American bases in Japan sustained U.S. operations during the Korean War and later during the Vietnam War. Now paid for by the Japanese, they remain essential for supporting Korea, Thailand, Taiwan, or the Philippines in the event of future hostilities. The U.S. cannot hope to confront China successfully if it gives up its Japanese connection and its bases on Japanese soil.[12]

With a world-class economy, Japan clearly possesses the wherewithal to be a major geostrategic player. Yet it eschews any dominant political role even within its East Asian homeland, and possesses only a modest defense capability, preferring to operate in concert with America and under its protection. The U.S. must carefully nurture the American-Japanese relationship, encouraging Japan in the direction of closer military cooperation with the U.S., with a view to jointly protecting U.S. and Japanese interests in the region from expanding Chinese threats. The Japanese parliament's May 1999 passage of defense guidelines, aimed at facilitating cooperation between U.S. and Japanese forces in unspecified "areas surrounding Japan," was an important step in this direction.

Taiwan is also critical to thwarting Chinese hegemony. Its buoyant democracy and thriving economy—it is our seventh largest trading partner—make it an important player in its own right. A more effective response to China's 1996 "missile diplomacy" than sending two carriers into harm's way would have been to open an official consulate on Taiwan immediately, informing Beijing that the next time it engaged in such overtly aggressive acts, the U.S. would promptly extend diplomatic recognition to the island democracy. This would have lessened the chance of a military clash by keeping our carriers at a safe remove, while at the same time making clear to Beijing that any use of force against Taiwan would be counterproductive because it would result in a great leap forward in Taiwan's international stature.

In the meantime, we should strengthen Taiwan's defenses. Current restrictions on arms sales to Taiwan should be lifted, to boost the island's ability to defend itself. Taiwan should be provided with key weapons systems, including theater missile defenses, to help offset the growing Chinese missile threat across the Strait. The ban on high-level military exchanges between our two countries should be ended, which would allow planning on the defense of Taiwan to go forward.

Only a firm U.S. commitment to the defense of Taiwan and decisive U.S. action in case of aggression can forestall a military invasion by Beijing in the years to come. "I do not believe in a peaceful transition," Chairman Mao told Kissinger in 1973, referring to the recovery of Taiwan. His successors apparently do not either, as the recent threat by the PRC to use force to effect reunification with the island demonstrates.[13]

PEACEFUL EVOLUTION

Just by containing China, by preventing a military breakout, we help to channel that country's energies into economic development, and thus bring about change. But if we want to ensure that liberty has an opportunity to flourish along with the economy, we must work not only to slow down China's militarization but also to speed up its democratization, allowing political development to catch up to economic and military modernization.

Having witnessed the stunning collapse of communist regimes in Central Europe and the former Soviet Union, China's leaders realize how quickly the fabric of their control could unravel if ordinary people felt free to dissent from official policy. Their worst fear is a successful, large-scale reprise of the Tiananmen demonstrations: a sudden and complete paralysis of their regime by a spontaneous mass movement, resulting in its peaceful overthrow. Their nightmare should be our foreign policy goal: the peaceful evolution of China from a one-party dictatorship practicing lawless coercion into a democratic state operating under the rule of law.

The phrase "peaceful evolution" comes from a speech, long-forgotten in the West, by John Foster Dulles. In 1959 the then-secretary of state conceded to an audience at the Commonwealth Club in San Francisco that the United States could not "roll back" communism by military force. Henceforth, he said, the U.S. would work to evolve communist dictatorships into democracies by softer methods, such as trade and educational and cultural exchanges. From the U.S. perspective, this shift from a policy of rollback to one of peaceful evolution marked a retreat. Chairman Mao, however, read it differently, seeing in it a sophisticated new plan to subvert communism by non-military means, a prospect that frightened him and the rest of the Chinese leadership perhaps more than a military exchange with the U.S. After all, he had fought the U.S. to a draw in Korea.

Time would reveal that Chairman Mao was giving us credit for far more sophistication and consistency in our foreign policy than we actually possessed. Neither Dulles nor any of his successors sought to put in place a coherent policy of peaceful evolution vis-à-vis China. In fact, it would be over three decades before another secretary of state publicly proposed one. Not until 1993, reflecting the post-Tiananmen revulsion toward the Chinese leadership, did Warren Christopher suggest that the U.S. actively seek the end of communist rule in China. "Our policy will be to seek to facilitate a broad, peaceful evolution in China from communism to democracy," Clinton's first secretary of state testified during his confirmation hearings, "by encouraging the forces of economic and political liberalization in that great and highly important country."[14]

Christopher's remarks elicited a stern rebuke from Foreign Ministry spokesman Wu Jianmin, who warned the U.S. not to interfere in China's internal affairs. Later, when Christopher traveled to Beijing, he received what was arguably the coldest reception ever accorded a visiting American official. Being seen by the Chinese as a "peaceful evolutionist" and not as a pliable practitioner of realpolitik may have accounted for part of the chill.

What would a policy of peaceful evolution entail?

Promoting Human Rights

China's human rights record is indefensible. The state routinely arrests, imprisons and even tortures those who speak out against government policies or call for democratization. The publishers of underground publications, the Chinese version of Samizdat, are hunted down and arrested. There is no freedom of assembly, as the Tiananmen massacre demonstrated to the world in 1989, nor of association, as the Falun Gong arrests proved in 1999. Up to one hundred million Christians risk their lives daily by defying government orders banning free worship. The annual State Department "China Country Report," chronicling the latest extrajudicial executions, forced abortions, and other such crimes against humanity, makes for grim reading.[15]

The rights codified in the United Nations Charter on Human Rights and other international documents are intended for the protection of all mankind, not just Americans. The Beijing regime is a signatory to those documents, and it should be forcefully reminded that, if it fails to abide by them, then normal relations in trade and other areas will be impossible.

Trade should always be linked to human rights in dealings with our principal adversary. As during our four-decades-long contest with the Soviet Union, the stakes are too high to let our foreign policy be driven solely by profit. The Jackson-Vanik Amendment, which linked trade with the Soviet Union to free emigration from that country, was an effective way of highlighting U.S. principles. Most Americans, who in polls rank concerns about China's human rights record and growing military might well above trade, will applaud the application of a similar policy to the People's Republic.

Human rights and national security, often viewed as antithetical interests, are actually complementary. Human rights are the building blocks of democracy, which in turn is the surest guarantee of peace. The freedoms at issue (speech, press, religion, assembly, etc.) are the stepping stones to political participation, gradual pluralization and eventual democratization. The *Samizdat* newsletter of today is the opposition newspaper of tomorrow; the political dissident of today is the political candidate of tomorrow.

There is little doubt that the rise of popular sovereignty in China would lead China to moderate, if not entirely abandon, its hegemonic ambitions. Whatever future frictions may arise between a democratically governed China and the U.S., it is unlikely that an elected government in Beijing would resort to force to resolve them. It is a truism but true nonetheless: Democratic nations do not make war on each other.

From 1989 to 1993, as Director of the Asian Studies Center at the Claremont Institute, I and other Institute personnel organized a dozen or more symposia for Chinese pro-democracy leaders. We were eager to help educate them in the principles of liberty and the mechanics of democracy. We taught them Robert's Rules of Order so they could debate political issues in an atmosphere free of fear and chaos. We distributed Chinese translations of the U.S. Constitution. We encouraged discussion on the principles of self-government. In this effort we were, to judge from the positive response of the symposia participants, largely successful.

At the same time, we realized that unless such democratic structures could rest securely on a historical and cultural foundation, they would not long survive. So we went back to the works of Confucius, Mencius, the Legalists, and others, hoping to find references, however oblique, to such concepts as popular sovereignty, separation of powers, and the like. In this effort we were by and large disappointed. There was no tradition of respect for human rights, indeed, no notion of inalienable rights at all, in the Chinese classics. There was certainly no ghost of a suggestion that government in any way derived its just powers from the consent of the governed. From the beginning of Chinese recorded history, the emperor had been an absolute despot. In this regard, there was little to choose between Qin Shihuang, who ruled 221–206 B.C., and Mao Zedong, who ruled A.D. 1949–1975. China's autocratic traditions provided no hospitable soil into which to transplant the foreign roots of democracy.

The naive assumption that China's continued economic development will shortly give rise to a participatory democracy is just that: naive. While economic expansion and trade are essential for the growth of middle and entrepreneurial classes, the mere existence of such classes does not translate inevitably into political reform. In both Taiwan and Hong Kong, economic development and the rule of law brought in its wake demands for liberalization, but with very different results. A dictatorial, Legalist-oriented government in Beijing has kept Hong Kong's democratic aspirations bottled up, perhaps permanently. A sympathetic, Western-oriented government on Taiwan acceded to such demands in the 80s, and the island today enjoys a multiparty democracy.

Taiwan as Precursor

Taiwan is more than just a success story for democracy. Viewed in the context of Greater China, this flash point of Asia, this constant irritant to U.S.-China relations ironically enough offers a way out of China's century and a half of political travail.

The forces that were to culminate in a democratic Taiwan were born in the closing decades of the nineteenth century in China's great coastal cities. The failing Qing dynasty was growing too weak to enforce its oppressive, Legalist laws. In the public space created by this impotence, the first seeds of Chinese civil society began to sprout. Newspapers sprang up, "educational and study groups" were formed, and the first modern Chinese universities were founded.[16] In 1905 Sun Yat-sen set up his Revolutionary Alliance (Tongmenghui), which called for the overthrow of the Qing dynasty and the establishment of a constitutional republic. Its charter promised representative government and equal treatment before the law.[17]

With the collapse of the Qing dynasty in 1911, the Republic of China was established. It was self-consciously modeled upon the United States, with its separation of powers and a presidential, rather than parliamentary, political system. Almost ten percent of the Chinese population voted in the first election, a level of popular participation in the electoral process which was not achieved by Japan until 1928 and by India until 1935.[18]

The weak Republican government proved unable to restrain the former Qing generals and provincial governors, and China promptly descended into two and a half decades of warlordism. The absence of central authority, however, gave even greater scope to China's nascent civil society, which continued to flourish. Chiang Kai-shek, who unified much of China under the banner of the Nationalist Party in 1928, did not attempt to reimpose the outdated strictures of Legalism. Rather, he devoted great energy to preparing a comprehensive legal code based on continental European law, and to building up an efficient government administration in accordance with Sun Yat-sen's principles. The Chinese people took advantage of their new freedoms of the press and assembly to start new publications and newspapers, form voluntary associations, and organize institutions of higher education. By 1946 there were some 1,200 voluntary associations of various kinds, and 200 colleges and universities with a total enrollment of 155,000.[19]

During the decades of Nationalist rule, a panoply of groups and institutions autonomous from the state emerged in China. This proto–civil society included representative assemblies, privately owned media, private institutions of higher learning, independent academic societies and voluntary associations. Despite—or perhaps because of—the pressures of upstart warlords, the Japanese invasion, official corruption and, towards the end of that period, an increasingly menacing communist movement, some fundamental political changes away from autocracy were occurring. In terms of its development of civil society and political participation, the Republic of China was far more "revolutionary" than the People's Republic of China that followed. This proto–civil society, a dozen political parties, a thriving press—all of this was destroyed when the Japanese invaded and the Chinese Communist Party came to power.

Do the Nationalists deserve any credit for the germination of a civil society in China? Or was it an unintended consequence of Nationalist corruption, ineptitude, or distraction? Let us consider the expressed intentions of the Nationalist Party's founder. Sun Yat-sen had articulated a vision of China's political development taking place in three steps: military rule, political tutelage, and constitutional government. Once the Nationalist armies had put an end to armed opposition, they would hand over authority to the Nationalist Party. The Party would exercise authority until the people had been properly "tutored" in the ways of representative government. The establishment of a constitutional government would mark the end of Party dictatorship, with the Kuomintang thereafter having to compete with other political parties for voter support in free and open elections.

It is easy to mock this open-ended commitment to representative government, which was little in evidence during the Japanese invasion and subsequent civil war, as being no more than an elaborate ideological justification for one-party rule. To those skeptical of political myths, be they Nationalist, Communist, or Confucian, the period of "political tutelage" was no more likely to come to an end than the state was to wither away under

communism, or the emperor to rule by mere force of moral example in the dynastic period. Yet the later history of Taiwan shows
that many of the KMT faithful took this promise seriously, including, in the end, the scion of the Chiang family himself, President
Chiang Ching-kuo. And we see the fruit of this development today
in Taiwan, the first Chinese state to break the Legalist stranglehold
of state control and achieve not only a full-blooded civil society,
but a thriving democracy.

While China was locked in the grip of a totalitarian regime
run by the megalomaniac Mao Zedong, Taiwan in the fifties and
sixties was busily gaining experience in local democracy, holding
election after election at the county and township level. A successful land reform and the encouragement of foreign trade led to
economic progress, which in turn promoted even greater contact
with the West. And over the past two decades, as the People's
Republic has developed its peculiar brand of Leninist capitalism,
the Republic of China has successfully made the transition from
autocratic state to modern democracy.

Cultural and political change were greatly accelerated in Taiwan,
a small island nation, not only because it was cut off from the mass
of China, but also because it was utterly dependent upon the United
States. Within such a context, the U.S. example of ordered liberty and respect for human rights carried the day, overwhelming
traditional notions of autocratic rule within a generation. Chiang
Ching-kuo was a very different kind of leader from his father,
Chiang Kai-shek; he tolerated dissent rather than trying to eliminate it, and even quietly accepted, near the end of his life, the
formation of a competing political party.

The Republican revolution of 1911 succumbed to a Communist
counterrevolution on the mainland, but ultimately succeeded on
Taiwan. Although the Chinese Communist Party won the military
contest in 1949, the Nationalists have won the peace in the half-
century since. By every measure of human well-being, from per
capita GNP to respect for human rights, Taiwan stands head and
shoulders above the mainland. There are few on either side of the
Taiwan Strait who would deny this.

And so the best defense against the Hegemon is not to be found just in the erection of missile defense systems, the expansion of the Seventh Fleet, or even the strengthening of Asian alliances. All these are important, and cannot be neglected. But the best defense is, quite simply, the continued existence of a stable, democratic, and prosperous Taiwan. By its powerful example of ordered liberty, it contradicts the Communist Party's claim to be the sole alternative to chaos in China. With its first-world living standards, it exposes the continued poverty of Market Leninism. Taiwan, in short, is not just a parallel universe coexisting uneasily with an evil twin, but rather a road map to what could one day exist in all of China. This is why it is under threat. This is why it must be protected.

THE END OF THE HEGEMON

Standing at a crossroads in our China policy, we must be wary of an overreaction that would produce the very belligerence we hope to contain. Yet in dealing with the Hegemon, underreaction or inconstancy creates an even greater danger.

Wuwei adherents proclaim that China is a friendly, nonaligned nation, one that will never endanger our interests or those of our friends; yet their actions say the opposite. We need do nothing to contain China, they assert, while quietly approving arms sales to Taiwan. China's democratic evolution will occur naturally, they claim, but then skewer Chinese officials in private meetings over human rights abuses. This is the worst of policy worlds, for it results in doing just enough to anger the Communist elite and keep them on edge, but not enough either to constrain their ambitions or to promote China's democratic evolution.

Other China watchers acknowledge that China is *at present* fundamentally undemocratic and hostile toward U.S. power, but believe this state of affairs is merely temporary. The U.S. should not overreact, they argue, because economic modernization and foreign contacts will bring freedom to China within the next few years. We simply have to maintain our current force levels in Asia, remain on good terms with our existing allies, make clear our intention to defend Taiwan against aggression, and await the flowering of representative government in the People's Republic.

But China is not just hostile toward U.S. power; rather, by its own account, it is actively seeking to replace that power with Chinese hegemony. Beijing's military prowess—and its belligerence—will continue to grow apace. Its nuclear arsenal, useful mainly for posturing and blustering at present, will become a formidable attack weapon. The military technology gap will close, and China will have the ability to project force over long distances. Its economy will rival that of the U.S. in size.

As China's power grows, the fear it inspires among dovish westerners will drive more into the appeasement camp. For some time to come, America will remain much wealthier, technologically advanced, and militarily adept than the PRC, though under a policy of appeasement these advantages cannot be realized until the advent of open conflict, by which time the asymmetries will have largely disappeared.

At the present moment, American still stands supreme. Our military has global reach, our economy is the envy of the world, our technology remains cutting edge, and our democratic ideals have worldwide appeal. We are the only power in the world capable of stopping the Hegemon. But our policy is currently frozen in the amber of outdated assumptions about China, rendering us unable to act in accordance with our continuing stark ideological differences, still dreaming that strategic partnership with the communist giant is necessary and even desirable.

As a distant maritime power with no territorial ambitions, the U.S. should avoid hubris, shoulder its responsibility, and do the best it can to continue the present *Pax Americana*.[20] A failure to acknowledge this burden or, worse yet, a retreat into isolationism would only encourage aggression on the part of would-be competitors like China. In the end, as in World War I and World War II, the U.S. would be forced to intervene, but at a high cost in blood and treasure.

The Great Game of the twenty-first century will be between the United States and China. America's success in this competition will reaffirm its role as the leading state in the West, foster unity with a global network of democratic allies, and demonstrate once and for all the universality of human rights and representative government. The peaceful evolution of China into a democratic state would be the final, and greatest, triumph of the American experiment in representative government.

The triumph of democracy in China would be a victory not just for the United States and its founding ideals, but for the Chinese people as well. They would at last throw off the shackles of totalitarianism over two millennia after they were forged by the First Hegemon of the Qin dynasty, and complete the democratic journey they began in 1911 with the overthrow of the Manchu dynasty and have achieved under difficult circumstances on the island of Taiwan. No goal could be more worthy than this: to bring these two great peoples, the Americans and the Chinese—so alike in many ways, so different in their current forms of governance—together once and for all.

Afterword

When the Chinese government declared me to be an "international spy" twenty years ago, after I had written a series of articles on human rights violations in the PRC, the silence from the U.S. China-watching community was deafening. Instead of expressing outrage over this absurd charge leveled at one of their own, my colleagues one by one distanced themselves, each afraid that by voicing support he or she would be singled out for punishment by the Beijing regime—punishment in this case being denial of access. "Your case threatens to make it more difficult for the rest of us to go to China and do research," wrote one senior China hand whose support I had been counting on.

There will probably always be China watchers who trim their sails for fear that Beijing will withhold visas or approval for research projects. Recently, for example, one Washington-based analyst expressed great interest in a "Human Rights in China" conference my institute was organizing, but then, in response to my invitation, decided he couldn't possibly be present at such a gathering. "I prefer to keep my channels of communication to Beijing open," he said with a grimace.

But such a willingness to pander to Beijing is gradually becoming less common. There is a steadier, more realistic view among the professionals than there was nearly thirty years ago when Nixon made his opening. At that time there was an air of such heady enthusiasm among China-watchers, people who were supposed to know better, that they resembled Lincoln Steffens and a prior generation who had seen the future and saw that it works. Now, a soberer view prevails.

159

Fewer China watchers are willing to remain silent when the truth about, say, China's persecution of Christians is distorted or denied by the government, or when one of their number is savaged for reporting it. Nowadays, the arrest of American scholars is likely to generate not silence but public criticism from the Sinological community. For instance, when Song Yongyi, a librarian at Dickinson College in Carlisle, Pennsylvania, was arrested in August 1999 on charges of illegally collecting information about the Cultural Revolution, dozens of China hands signed a petition calling for his release. This raised the price of his incarceration too high for Beijing, and eventually he was released.

There is a lesson here on larger issues. It is time for the Great Wall of intimidation that the Hegemon has built up around itself to come tumbling down. America's response to the challenge posed by China rests in large part on the willingness of American Sinologists to write without fear or favor. If the China watchers get it right, then the American public and policy makers will, too. And on this hinges our future.

Many China watchers, among others, helped me with this book, reading all or part of the manuscript at various stages and making many useful comments and suggestions: Nicholas Eberstadt, Zhengyuan Fu, Miriam London, Ambassador James Lilley, Robert Hickson, Ian Haynes, Ron Pandolfi, Larry Arnn, Bruce Herschensohn, Al Santoli, Bill Saunders, Dana Rohrabacher, Rick Fisher, Vince Cruz, Chuck DeVore, Constantine Menges, John Delmare, Christopher Manion, Ben Tang, and others who, by their own request, must go unnamed. While I am grateful to all who graciously helped along the way, I must claim sole responsibility for any errors that remain.

Finally, I must thank my executive assistant, Sarah Dateno, who labored with me through several drafts, and my indefatigable editor, Peter Collier, who insisted that the words of *Hegemon* must fall into place, in George Orwell's phrase, as gracefully "as coins into slots."

Notes

[1] Bureaucratic totalitarianism is often thought to be an invention of the twentieth century, an evil alchemy of 19th-century Marxist ideology and 20th-century Leninist bureaucracy capable of transmuting precious freedoms into base slavery. But the inventor of the iron cage of totalitarianism was not Vladimir Ilyich Lenin—though it is of course his specter that loomed over the peoples of Central and Eastern Europe for so many decades—but the founding emperor of the Qin dynasty, Qin Shihuang, and his Legalist Machiavelli, Li Si.

[2] In a recent paper published by the London-based International Institute for Strategic Studies, Japanese foreign ministry analyst Koro Bessho writes, "The Middle Kingdom was not simply Asia's largest state, but the world itself. . . . In theory, there were no boundaries between the Empire and neighboring nations, which were seen as little more than 'barbarian' lands owing different levels of allegiance to the Emperor." Koro Bessho, "Identities and Security in East Asia," Adelphi Paper 325 (London: International Institute for Strategic Studies, March 1999).

[3] Ross H. Munro, "Eavesdropping on the Chinese Military: Where it Expects War—Where it Doesn't," *Orbis* (Summer, 1994): 1–17.

[4] China's tradition of hegemony implies a preexisting claim on the loyalties, if not the territory, of neighboring vassal and tributary states. So it was that even Chiang Kai-shek could write, "After having witnessed the tragedy of the loss of the Liuchiu Islands [Ryukyus], Hong Kong, Formosa [Taiwan], the Pescadores, *Annam [Vietnam], Burma and Korea,* China was confronted with the great danger of imminent partition of her entire territory" (italics added). Chiang Kai-shek, *China's Destiny* (New York: MacMillan, 1947), 34; see also 242 n. 19.

[5] For these and many similar comments, see Michael Pillsbury, ed., *China Debates the Future Security Environment* (Washington, D.C.: National Defense University Press, 2000).

[6] Song Yimin, "A Discussion of the Division and Grouping of Forces in the World after the End of the Cold War" (in Chinese), *Renmin Ribao* (People's Daily), 29 April 1996. A longer version of this article originally appeared in

the journal *International Studies* (Beijing: China Institute of International Studies) 6, no. 8 (1996): 10.

[7] Zbigniew Brzezinski, *The Grand Chessboard: American Primacy and its Geostrategic Imperatives* (New York: Basic Books, 1997), 170. The most accessible translation of Sun-tzu's thought is by Ralph D. Sawyer, *The Complete Art of War* (Boulder, Colorado: Westview Press, 1996).

[8] *China's National Defense,* white paper issued by the Information Office of the State Council, the People's Republic of China, 27 July 1998, 1. This white paper is available from the Chinese Embassy's web site at www.china-embassy.org.

[9] Ibid., 3.

[10] This formulation is not new. China has placed itself in opposition to the United States since at least August 1994, when Deng Xiaoping defined China's geostrategic goals as "First, to oppose hegemony and power politics and safeguard world peace; second, to build up a new international political and economic order."

[11] Brzezinski, *Grand Chessboard,* 172. The *People's Daily* had earlier condemned the increased scope of U.S.-Japan military cooperation as "a dangerous move." "Strengthening Military Alliance does not Conform with Trend of the Times" (in Chinese), *Renmin Ribao,* 31 January 1997.

[12] "China's National Defense," 5.

[13] Brzezinski, *Grand Chessboard,* 172.

[14] Ibid., 169. At the same time, there are tactical reasons for China's interest in a "strategic partnership" with America over the short to medium term, among them driving a wedge between the U.S. and its long-standing allies in the region, and providing cover for the transition to Chinese dominance.

[15] *Megatrends China* (Beijing: Hualing Publishing House, 1996); cited in Bruce Gilley, "Potboiler Nationalism," *Far Eastern Economic Review,* 3 October 1996. According to several selections in *China Debates the Future Security Environment,* the late Chinese leader Deng Xiaoping was the author of the military strategy of "biding our time and building up our capabilities."

[16] These examples come from Pillsbury, ed., *China Debates the Future Security Environment.*

CHAPTER TWO: Birth of the Hegemon

[1] In the following sections I draw heavily upon the seminal work of Professor Zhengyuan Fu, especially his *Autocratic Tradition and Chinese Politics* (Cambridge: Cambridge University Press, 1993) and *China's Legalists: The Earliest Totalitarians and Their Art of Ruling* (Armonk, New York: M. E. Sharpe, 1996). Despite the influence of their thought on Chinese history, the Legalists have been largely neglected by modern Sinology. John King Fairbank's *China: A New History* (Cambridge: Harvard University Press, 1992), for example, contains not a single reference to this pivotal school of statecraft.

[2] Hsu, C., *Ancient China in Transition* (Stanford: Stanford University Press, 1965), 58.

[3] While the chief Legalists reflected deeply on the nature of power and its employment, as a class the Legalists more closely resembled the *consiglieri* of Mafia chieftains, each plotting to advance the power of his boss against the other bosses.

[4] *Han Fei Zi*, chs. 47, 49, 50; cited in Fu, *Autocratic Tradition*, 20. Among the forerunners of Legalism was a branch of Daoism called the Huang-Lao school (school of the Yellow Emperor and Lao Zi). Through the Huang-Lao school, many Daoists prescriptions became Legalist statecraft. This connection came to light with the discovery of the *Huangdi sijing* (Four Canons of the Yellow Emperor) during a 1973 excavation of a Han dynasty tomb in Hunan province. The views expressed in this ancient document accord with those of the Legalists, for example: "Possessing a large territory, a teeming population, and a strong army, the ruler is matchless in the world." See Fu, *Autocratic Tradition*, 37.

[5] Charles O. Hucker, *China's Imperial Past* (Stanford: Stanford University Press, 1975), 92.

[6] Max Weber defined power as "the probability that one actor within a social relationship will be in a position to carry out his own will despite resistance, regardless of the basis on which this probability rests." Weber, *The Theory of Social and Economic Organizations*, trans. A. M. Henderson and Talcott Parsons (New York: The Free Press, 1947), 152.

[7] Those Legalists who successfully implemented their programs thus ran a risk of execution, and at least two Legalist chancellors (Shang Yang and Wu Qi) so met their deaths. Hsu, *Ancient China*, 38–52.

[8] The Great Wall of China as we know it today was built by the Ming dynasty in the sixteenth century, as Arthur Waldron has conclusively shown in *The Great Wall of China: From History to Myth* (Cambridge: Cambridge University Press, 1990). Earlier walls were built by Qin, other Warring States, and later dynasties.

[9] Li Si, "Memorial on the Burning of Books," *Shi Ji* 87:6b–7a, translated in *Sources of Chinese Tradition*, ed. Theodore de Bary, Wing-tsit Chan, and Burton Watson (New York: Columbia University Press, 1960), 154–155.

[10] Derk Bodde, in vol. 1 of the *Cambridge History of China*, suggests that the 460 (not 463) scholars were not actually buried alive, only murdered, and that the mistake follows from a mistranslation; but this is a minority view.

[11] There are those who would argue, even in the face of all this evidence, that the Qin state was not truly totalitarian since it was not able to achieve total control over the entire range of human thought and action. But this is like saying that the U.S. is not truly democratic because not everyone votes in elections. Totalitarianism, like democracy, is an ideal type, the real-world facsimile of which can scarcely be without deficiencies. Intentions must be weighed alongside results. And the intent of the First Emperor of the Qin dynasty, few would dispute, was to totally dominate his subjects. The Legalist system

of government that he employed for that purpose came as close to achieving total control over the population as the relatively primitive means of communication and transportation then allowed, and can properly be judged totalitarian.

[12] See H. G. Creel, *Chinese Thought: From Confucius to Mao Tse-tung* (Chicago: University of Chicago Press, 1953), esp. chap. 9; Hsiao Kung-chuan, *Zhongguo zhengzhi sixiang shi* (A history of Chinese political thought) (Taipei: Linking, 1982); and Arthur Wright, *Chinese Thought and Institutions* (1957), 85. "By the time the Legalists had completed their work of sabotage," Creel astutely concludes, "the true nature of Confucius had been thoroughly obscured." (237–241) Respect for the inviolability and integrity of the sacred texts of Chinese history had given way before the political exigencies of succeeding dynasties. The official ideology of Imperial China was not "Confucian" so much as a clever amalgam of Legalist principles and Confucian rhetoric.

[13] Because many elements of Legalist political philosophy are traceable to Daoism through the Huang-Lao school, some Chinese historians assert that traditional Chinese political philosophy is a mixture of Confucianism and Daoism.

[14] Fu, *Autocratic Traditions*, 35. For most of the past 2,000 years, the Chinese state loudly proclaimed its adherence to moral principles that it rarely observed in practice.

[15] Some rulers, of course, were more cunning practitioners of the Confucian-Legalist deceit than others. As PRC Marxist historian Fan Wenlan writes, "Following the Qin and Han periods, those emperors of succeeding dynasties who knew how to employ Confucianism on the outside but applied Daoism [of the Legalist variety] on the inside, that is, blending the Way of Sage Kings with that of the Hegemon, saw their reigns prosper. Those who were not adept at this saw their reigns decline." Fan Wenlan, *Zhongguo tongshi* (A general history of China) (Beijing: Renmin chubanshe, 1978), vol. 1, 248; cited in Fu, *Autocratic Traditions*, 62.

[16] China Proper, as commonly defined, is "a roughly square land mass about half the size of the continental United States, bounded on the north by the Great Wall, on the west by Inner Asian wastelands and Tibetan highlands, and on the south and east by oceans. This is the historical Chinese homeland." See Charles O. Hucker, *China's Imperial Past* (Stanford: Stanford University Press, 1975), 2.

[17] I offer a population figure with some trepidation. As the eminent Israeli ancient historian Ben Isaac has written recently, "Demography is one of those topics which are as important as they are frustrating to those interested in the ancient world. The absence of information is such that modern specialists consider any effort at serious study an idle undertaking." See Isaac, "Jews, Christians and Others in Palestine: The Evidence from Eusebius," in *Jews in a Graeco-Roman World*, ed. M. Goodman (Oxford: Clarendon Press, 1998), 65. Some scholars have, nevertheless, attempted to estimate the size of the empire's population, and occasionally a figure of 60 million is mentioned. Ian Haynes has written, "I am pretty convinced that this is too low. What makes

such estimates so doubtful is the basis on which they are calculated and the way in which local studies repeatedly suggest higher population levels than those once suspected. Britain, one of the most intensely studied provinces, offers an example of this phenomenon. Up until recently, scholars tended to imagine that the population stood at around 2 million (approximately twice the generally accepted estimate for the Iron Age population at the beginning of the 1st millennium B.C.). Now scholars talk of figures of 6 to 8 million, after field survey and aerial reconnaissance reveal the existence of much denser settlement patterns. At the same time, prehistorians have started to question their earlier estimates, observing not only much denser settlement, but also that far higher agricultural yields were possible with Iron Age farming methods than was hitherto believed." Personal correspondence with the author, 29 February 2000. For the size of the Roman army, see John Wacher, ed., *The Roman World* (London, Boston: Routledge & K. Paul, 1987), 3.

[18] Although summary records of Han dynasty censuses survive intact to the present day, they count only households, so one has to use a somewhat controversial multiplier to reach the generally accepted figure of 59.5 million in A.D. 2. The Han dynasty was able to maintain such a large number of men under arms by practicing conscription, with all able-bodied males in the country obliged to serve for two years. Convicts and volunteers provided additional sources of manpower.

[19] The brief Sui dynasty (519–618) was immediately succeeded by the Tang (618–906), without an appreciable interregnum.

[20] Etienne Balazs, *Chinese Civilization and Bureaucracy* (New Haven: Yale University Press, 1964), 10.

CHAPTER THREE: **The Hegemon Reawakens**

[1] Mao Zedong, " 'Friendship' or Aggression," *Selected Works of Mao Tse-tung*, vol. 4 (Beijing: Foreign Language Press, 1969), 447–49. This speech was a response to the U.S. State Department's white paper on China, formally called *United States Relations with China*, and Secretary of State Dean Acheson's "Letter of Transmittal" of same to President Truman, both of which were published on August 5, 1949.

[2] Mao Zedong, *Mao Zhuxi shici sanshiqi shi* (Thirty-seven poems of Chairman Mao) (Beijing: Renmin chubanshe, 1964). Translation by the author.

[3] Mao Zedong, *Selected Works*, vol. 4, 195; cited in Fu, *Autocratic Tradition*, 188. Some sources have 46 thousand instead of 460 thousand.

[4] During the Cultural Revolution, PLA Marshal Peng Dehuai told the Red Guards who were persecuting him that "Comrade Mao Zedong is more familiar with Chinese history than anyone else in the Party. The first emperor of a dynastic era was always very wise, and very ferocious." Wang Xizhe, "On Socialist Democracy," in *On Socialist Democracy and the Chinese Legal System*, eds. A. Chan, Stanley Rosen, and J. Unger (Armonk, New York: Sharpe, 1985).

[5] Stuart Schram, ed., *Chairman Mao Talks to the People* (New York: Random House, 1974).

[6] V. Holubnychy, "Mao Tse-tung's Materialistic Dialectics," *China Quarterly* 19 (July–September 1964).

[7] Mao Zedong and the Chinese Communist Party had adopted a pose as "agrarian reformers" during the last decade of the Chinese civil war, advocating a "New Democracy" in local governance and promising to rule "democratically" when they came to power. But as Nationalist resistance collapsed in early 1949 and a Chinese Communist Party victory appeared certain, Mao decided the time had come to abandon this pretense. The new national government would not be a democracy after all, he declared on 1 July 1949, but a "people's democratic dictatorship."

[8] The Chinese Communist party led "a counterrevolution against the first Chinese republican revolution of 1911," argues Professor Zhengyuan Fu, and following its victory restored a revitalized traditional autocracy. Fu, *Autocratic Tradition*, 2. Former President Lee Teng-Hui of Taiwan holds a similar view: "What did the Communist revolution accomplish? It did not bring the continent out of stagnation or free the people of stifling, oppressive tradition; what it did do was resurrect "hegemony" and imperialism." Lee Teng-hui, *The Road to Democracy: Taiwan's Pursuit of Identity* (Tokyo: PHP Institute, 1999), 53.

[9] Mao was characteristically blunt about his aims. Under the guidance of the Chinese Communist Party, the masses would exercise a "democratic dictatorship," whose first and most important task would be to liquidate bad or "antagonistic" classes, defined as "the running dogs of imperialism—the landlord class [and] the bureaucrat-bourgeoisie, as well as the representatives of those classes, the Kuomintang reactionaries and their accomplices." Eventually all class distinctions would cease to exist, Mao promised, but before that could happen these two "antagonistic" classes had to be "eliminated." Nor was Mao coy about how this class war was to be prosecuted. "Our present task is to strengthen the people's state apparatus," he wrote. "The state apparatus, including the army, the police and the courts, is the instrument by which one class oppresses another. It is an instrument for the oppression of antagonistic classes." Interestingly, Mao still felt obliged to pay lip service to democracy. "The people" would "enjoy freedoms of speech, assembly, association," and would have the right to vote and "elect their own government." But only on one condition: none of this was to interfere with the primary task of the new government, which was to exercise a dictatorship over the enemies of the people. It did not take a political philosopher to see that, even if the rights enumerated by Mao were inalienable, the right to membership in "the people" was not. Those who vigorously exercised their freedom of speech (or assembly, or association), or took seriously their right to "elect their own government," would run the risk of being declared "enemies of the people" by the state apparatus, who would then punish, imprison, or execute them with impunity. Mao Zedong, "On the People's Democratic Dictatorship," in *Selected Works*, vol. 4, 417–18.

[10] Personal conversation, 28 August 1998.

[11] This would not be the only time that Stalin attempted to restrain Mao. At the end of 1947, when the Red Army had swept the field in North China, Stalin suggested to Mao that he not cross the Yangtze to finish off the Nationalist armies in the south. "Stalin wanted to prevent China from making revolution," Mao later recalled, "saying we should not have a civil war and should cooperate with Chiang Kai-shek, otherwise the Chinese nation would perish. But we did not do what he said. The revolution was victorious. . . . After the victory of the revolution [Stalin] next suspected China of being a Yugoslavia, and that I would become a second Tito." Here Mao must have had his tongue firmly in cheek, for he had always been "a Tito." Despite his public posture of deference to Stalin, he was privately determined not to allow Soviet bases or troops on Chinese soil. Mao Zedong, "Speech at the Tenth Plenum of the Eighth Central Committee," 24 September 1962, reprinted in Schram, *Chairman Mao Talks,* 191.

[12] Mao Zedong, "Talks at the Chengdu Conference," March 1958, reprinted in Schram, *Chairman Mao Talks,* 101. Mao also complained about the Soviets' two "colonies" of the Northeast and Xinjiang. Although under Chinese control, the Soviets had insisted upon retaining special privileges in these two border regions, where people of any third country were not allowed to reside.

[13] Stalin seems to have taken a softer line in China than in Eastern Europe, deciding in the end not to bind it to the Soviet Union by force, but by economic aid and compromise. Still, given Mao's assertive nationalism, even Stalin's uncharacteristically velvet-glove approach would have failed within a few years had it not been for the outbreak of hostilities on the Korean Peninsula, which reforged the Sino-Russian alliance in the crucible of war, delaying for a decade the Sino-Soviet split.

[14] Samuel Wells, "The Lessons of the Korean War," in *The Korean War: a 25-Year Perspective,* ed. Francis Heller (Kansas, 1977). Although Russia was in the process of giving back much of this territory, other irritants remained. Outer Mongolia remained a Soviet puppet state, having been detached from China in the twenties. Much of the Russian Far East and Central Asia had also once been Chinese territory. Even more important was China's resurgent ambition—which Acheson, viewing China at its nadir, would perhaps have had difficulty taking seriously—to resume its proper place as the Hegemon.

[15] Those who believe that the Communist Party Chairman was frightened by the thought of American forces reaching his borders should consider that those forces at the time numbered only 200,000, scarcely enough to undertake the conquest of a continent guarded by four million battle-hardened PLA troops. Even at its peak strength in July 1953, the UN Command stood at 932,539 ground forces. Republic of Korea (ROK) army and marine forces accounted for 590,911 of that force, and U.S. Army and Marine forces for another 302,483. By comparison, other U.N. ground forces totaled some 39,145 men, 24,085 of whom were provided by British Commonwealth Forces (Great Britain, Canada, Australia and New Zealand) and 5,455 of whom came from Turkey. See Harry G. Summers, "The Korean War: A Fresh Perspective," *Military History* 13 (April 1996), 1.

[16] Schram, *Chairman Mao Talks*, 128. Even today, PLA generals boast of their "victories" over the United States. Take Lieutenant General Li Jijun, Vice-President of the PRL's Academy of Military Science, who has written, "To fight against a superior force and win victory is the highest honor for our army. From the end of the Second World War to the Gulf War, the United States fought two local wars, the Korean War and the Vietnam War, and in both suffered defeat. In both, its opponent was China. In the Korean War, it was the direct opponent, and in the Vietnam War, it was the indirect opponent. . . . To fight against a superior force and win victory is the highest honor for our army." Li Jijun, "Notes on Military Theory and Military Strategy," in *Chinese Views of Future Warfare*, ed. Michael Pillsbury, 2d ed. (Washington, D.C.: National Defense University Press, 1998), 230.

[17] John Gittings, *The World and China*, 1922–75 (London: Eyre Methuen, 1974), 236. Mao Zedong, "Talks at the Chengdu Conference: On the Problem of Stalin," March 1958, in Schram, *Chairman Mao Talks*, 98–99. Mao also began quietly questioning the way the Soviet "Elder Brothers" treated other countries within the communist bloc. When unrest broke out in Poland and Hungary following Khrushchev's anti-Stalin speech, he initially urged Khrushchev to withdraw all Soviet troops from these and other Eastern European countries. He mediated Polish-Soviet tensions following the election of reformer Wladyslaw Gomulka as Party first secretary, helping to prevent Soviet armed intervention. Lowell Dittmer, "China's Search for Its Place in the World," in *Contemporary Chinese Politics in Historical Perspective*, ed. Brantly Womack (Cambridge: Cambridge University Press, 1991), 213, based on a 1985 interview by the author with a member of the Institute of Soviet and Eastern European Studies in the Chinese Academy of Social Sciences in Beijing.

[18] Strobe Talbot, ed., *Khrushchev Remembers: The Last Testament* (Boston: Little, Brown, 1974), 269. Mao's pleasure over the signing of this agreement perhaps explains his mid-November visit to Moscow—his last. The occasion was a conference of leaders from communist countries to commemorate the fortieth anniversary of the October Revolution. Mao, not given to self-effacing remarks, declared at this event that "Our camp must have a head, because even a snake has a head. I would not agree that Chinese should be called head of the camp, because we do not merit this honor and cannot maintain this role, we are still poor. We haven't even a quarter of a satellite, while the Soviet Union has two. . . . The socialist camp is headed by the USSR." Quoted by Enver Hoxha, in *The Artful Albanian: Memoirs of Enver Hoxha*, ed. Jon Halliday (London: Chatto and Windus, 1986), 215.

[19] Indeed, just two months before he had told a meeting of the Military Affairs Commission that Chinese military theory and experience (which is to say, Mao's own) were superior to those of the Soviets.

[20] Talbot, *Khrushchev Remembers*, 269.

[21] Mao, "Speech at the Enlarged Session of the Military Affairs Committee and the External Affairs Conference," 11 September 1959, in Schram, *Chairman Mao Talks*, 151.

[22] At the Tenth Plenum of the Central Committee in 1962, Mao recalled his escalating troubles with Soviet leaders: "In 1958 Khrushchev wanted to set up a Soviet-Chinese combined fleet in order to seal us off [from attacking the offshore islands held by Taiwan]. At the time of the border dispute with India, he supported Nehru. At the dinner on our National Day he attacked us. . . . Today . . . we are called 'adventurists, nationalists, dogmatists.'" Mao's speech became public knowledge in the West only after it was published in 1969. Laszlo Ladany, *The Communist Party of China and Marxism: A Self-Portrait, 1921–1985* (Stanford: Hoover Institution Press, 1988), 267–68. Added to these insults was a real injury: Khrushchev's suspension of all technical assistance to China. Perhaps because Mao did not want to appear the supplicant, he did not mention that in 1960 Soviet engineers and technicians in China had rolled up their blueprints and returned home, cutting China off from its only source of modern technology.

[23] Ladany, *Communist Party of China*, 321. At the end of his speech, Lin Biao quoted Mao's great 1962 prophecy that within 50 to 100 years the world would go through a great transformation. Mao had not specified what the transformation would bring about, but it is likely that he meant China's return to greatness. *China News Analysis* (Hong Kong), no. 756.

[24] Beijing had been forced to take these steps, Zhou Enlai explained at the time, because Tibetan officials had "colluded with imperialism, assembled rebellious bandits, carried out rebellion," and—most incredibly of all—"put the Dalai Lama under duress." Zhou's claims were treated with the scorn they deserved. The U.S. State Department, on March 28, 1959, accused Communist China of a "barbarous intervention" and of attempting to "destroy the historical autonomy of the Tibetan people." Even the normally placid Nehru charged on March 30 that the Chinese Communists had broken pledges to allow Tibet "full autonomy." India sympathized with the Tibetan rebels, he said, and would admit refugees from Tibet on an individual basis.

[25] The Dalai Lama and his party of eighty officials, after an arduous 300-mile journey over the southern mountains of Tibet, reached India on March 31. He charged that Communist China was bent on the "complete absorption and extinction of the Tibetan race," and that 65,000 Tibetans had been slain since 1956. T. N. Schroth *et al.*, *China and U.S. Far East Policy, 1946–1967* (Washington, D.C.: Congressional Quarterly Series, 1967), 74–75, 92.

[26] The problem with these stories was that "there has been no systematic serfdom in Tibet for centuries. In 1879, an Indian scholar who had spent his life in the Himalayan area, Sarat Chandra Das, traveled to Lhasa and studied the social order. He found no trace of bonded servitude. He described a place (unlike caste-ridden India) where 'the rich may bestow their daughters on the poor; the daughter of a poor man may become the bride of the proudest noble in the country.' " Barbara Crossette, "The Shangri-la that Never Was," *New York Times*, 5 July 1998, 3.

[27] In April 1955, the Prime Ministers of Burma, Ceylon, India, Indonesia, and Pakistan invited a total of twenty-nine countries to an Asian-African Conference at Bandung in Indonesia. In addition to the sponsoring countries, there were Afghanistan, Cambodia, China, Egypt, Ethiopia, the Gold Coast, Iran, Iraq, Japan,

Jordan, Laos, Lebanon, Liberia, Libya, Nepal, the Philippines, Saudi Arabia, Sudan, Syria, Thailand, Turkey, North Vietnam, South Vietnam, and Yemen. The list included countries allied with the Western powers, Communist countries, and neutral countries. The list did not include the Republic of China on Taiwan, North and South Korea, and Israel, which were regarded as being too controversial, and South Africa, which was barred on the grounds of its racial policies. The conference provided a platform for the expression of anti-colonial sentiments, and several Asian leaders also made strong public statements against Communist imperialism.

[28] On September 4 an obviously nonplussed Nehru announced that the Chinese communists had accused India of "aggression" and demanded that India evacuate "Chinese territory." At first he indicated that he would be willing to make some minor adjustments to the border, and called the dispute "rather absurd." But Nehru was soon to admit that the Chinese claim was "much more serious" than he originally thought and "quite impossible for India ever to accept." He declared that India had "undertaken the defense of Sikkim and Bhutan, and anything that happens on their borders is the same as if it happened on the borders of India."

[29] This theory of *yuan jiao jin gong* was advocated by the Legalist scholar-strategist Fan Sui of the state of Qin during the Period of the Warring States (481–221 B.C.).

[30] Cited in H. C. Hinton, *China's Turbulent Quest* (New York: MacMillan, 1970), 67.

[31] D. D. Eisenhower, *Mandate for Change, 1953–56* (New York: Doubleday, 1963), 462–463.

[32] The Jinmen complex comprises Jinmen (Quemoy), Little Jinmen (Liehyu) and twelve islets. The total area of the Jinmen complex is 176.37 sq. km. As of 1971, Jinmen had a population of 61,008, not including military personnel. The Mazu Islands comprise Nangan and 18 other islets. The islands have an area of 27.1 sq. km. As of 1971, the civilian population was 17,057.

[33] Eisenhower's advisers were divided in their response to the Jinmen crisis. Some felt that the U.S. should pledge itself to defend the offshore islands and launch preemptive strikes. Of the members of the Joint Chiefs of Staff, Admiral Arthur W. Radford, Chairman of the Joint Chiefs of Staff; Admiral Robert B. Carney, Chief of Naval Operations; and General Nathan F. Twinning, the Air Force Chief of Staff urged that American and Nationalist Chinese planes be used to bomb Communist bases. General Matthew B. Ridgway, the Army Chief of Staff, opposed this action, saying any such action was likely to involve the United States in full-scale war. President Eisenhower sided with Ridgway. See N. M. Blake and O. T. Barck, *The United States in Its World Relations* (New York: McGraw Hill, 1960), 751.

[34] The Joint Resolution on the Defense of Formosa was passed by the House on a vote of 409 to 3 on February 26, and by the Senate two days later on a vote of 85 to 3. The resolution gave Eisenhower precisely what he wanted, authorization to "employ the Armed Forces of the United States for protecting the security of Formosa, the Pescadores, and related positions and territories of that

area." Both the threat faced by Taiwan and the vital American interest at stake were specified with admirable clarity: "[C]ertain territories in the West Pacific under the jurisdiction of the Republic of China are now under armed attack, and threats and declarations have been and are being made by the Chinese Communists that such armed attack is in aid of and in preparation for armed attack on Formosa and the Pescadores. . . . the secure possession by friendly governments of the Western Pacific Island chain, of which Formosa is a part, is essential to the vital interests of the United States and all friendly nations in or bordering upon the Pacific Ocean." Joint Resolution on Formosa, January 29, 1955, 84th Congress, 1st Session. *United States Statutes at Large*, vol. 69 (Washington, D.C.: Government Printing Office, 1955), 7.

[35] Dulles responded on April 26 by indicating his willingness to talk with the Chinese Communists about a cease-fire in the Taiwan Strait. He stressed that these talks would not imply official diplomatic recognition of the Chinese Communist regime, nor would the U.S. discuss the interests of the ROC "behind its back."

[36] Eisenhower, 482. The Geneva talks were upgraded from consular to ambassadorial level halfway through 1955, largely on the strength of a speech that Zhou Enlai had made all but promising to release 41 Americans detained by the PRC as "spies" and to renounce the use of force against Taiwan. Twelve were released over the months the followed, but Beijing sought to use the remaining 29 as bargaining chips. On September 10 Ambassador Wang Pingnan told Ambassador Johnson that all Americans would be released if the U.S. agreed to higher-level discussions. Johnson replied that the U.S. would consider the matter only after the Americans had actually been released. Schroth *et al.*, 74–75.

[37] D. D. Eisenhower, *Waging Peace: The White House Years, 1956–1961* (New York: Doubleday & Co., 1963), 556.

[38] President Eisenhower preferred that the Seventh Fleet merely patrol the Taiwan Strait rather than provide escorts for conveys. He assented to escort, however, with the proviso that American vessels should halt three miles off the unloading beaches, remaining in international waters. Frustrated in his plan to seize Jinmen by force, Mao fell back once more on political maneuvers, and requested talks with the U.S. Eisenhower, anxious to avoid a repetition of the explosive confrontation of September 7, agreed. On September 15 talks between the U.S. and the PRC were resumed in Warsaw after a hiatus of nearly a year. Dulles told a press conference that the odd and partial truce proved that "the killing is done for political purposes and promiscuously," and that the Communists "are trying to save themselves from a loss of face and a defeat in the effort which they had initiated but had been unable to conclude successfully." The ROC armed forces acquitted themselves well in the conflict. Thirty-one MiG-17s were shot down, 16 torpedo boats and gunboats were sunk, and a large number of PLA artillery batteries were destroyed. A total of 576,636 rounds of high explosives had fallen on Jinmen by November 22, resulting in some 3,000 civilian and 1,000 military casualties, and destroying many thousands of homes.

[39] The Great Leap Forward was actually part of a larger political campaign called *sanhongqi*—three red banners—referring to the general line of the Chinese Communist Party, the great leap forward and the people's communes.

[40] Eisenhower undertook a tour of East Asia, including the Republic of China on his itinerary. During his stay in Taipei, which began on June 18, 1960, he met twice with Chiang. The conversation ranged from ongoing security cooperation under the Sino-American Mutual Defense Treaty of 1954 to the international situation following the recent collapse of the Paris summit. Chiang emphasized the high priority that Soviet planners gave to East and Southeast Asia, which they viewed as the Achilles heel of the free world. The talks were satisfying and reassuring, with Eisenhower pledging the "steadfast solidarity" of the U.S. with the ROC. Eisenhower also gave a public address to a crowd of 65,000 people. The U.S. did not recognize the claim of the "warlike and tyrannical Communist regime" in Beijing to speak for all the Chinese people, he affirmed to thunderous cheers, promising that the U.S. would stand fast behind free China in resisting Communist aggression. As Eisenhower spoke, the Communist Chinese were saluting him in their own inimitable way. During the twenty-four hours Eisenhower was in Taipei, Quemoy was given its heaviest pounding ever by the PLA artillery batteries. An incredible 174,854 rounds fell upon the island. Eisenhower, *Waging Peace*, 564–565.

[41] Jonathan Wilkenfield, Michael Brecher, and Sheila Moser, eds., *Crises in the Twentieth Century*, vol. 2 (Oxford: Pergamon Press, 1988–89), 15, 161. Samuel P. Huntington, *The Clash of Civilizations and the Remaking of World Order* (New York: Simon & Shuster, 1996), 258.

CHAPTER FOUR: Great Han Chauvinism

[1] "Memorandum of Conversation between Chairman Mao Zedong and Secretary of State Henry Kissinger on 12 November 1973," in *The Kissinger Transcripts: The Top Secret Talks with Beijing and Moscow*, ed. William Burr (New York: The New Press, 1998), 187. This was not the only time that Mao protested Russian land grabs to Kissinger. At an earlier meeting, he spoke of how the Russians "didn't fire a single shot and yet they were able to grab so many places." While Premier Zhou Enlai chuckled ruefully in the background, he went on: "They grabbed the People's Republic of Mongolia. They grabbed half of Xinjiang. It was called their sphere of influence. And Manchukuo, on the northeast, was also called their sphere of influence." Ibid., 91.

[2] See, for instance, David S. G. Goodman, *Deng Xiaoping and the Chinese Revolution: A Political Biography* (London and New York: Routledge, 1994), 75.

[3] John Gittings, "New Material on Teng Hsiao-p'ing," *The China Quarterly* 67 (September 1975): 489.

[4] As James Mann has written, "[I]n 1989, the Chinese Communist Party was choosing a fundamentally different path from that of its counterparts in Eastern Europe and the Soviet Union. Rather than resort to violence, most of the other regimes were willing to share or, ultimately, give up power. The rulers

of China were not." Mann, "Debunking the Myths behind Tiananmen Crisis," *Los Angeles Times*, 2 June 1999.

⁵ See, for example, Richard Baum, *Burying Mao: Chinese Politics in the Age of Deng Xiaoping* (Princeton: Princeton University Press, 1994).

⁶ Jiang's differential handling of the two issues remains a befuddling inconsistency to some, leading editors to write subheads like "Who is China's president? For all Jiang's courage in securing the WTO deal, his handling of Falun Gong suggests fear is getting the better of his appetite for political reform." Susan V. Lawrence, "Jiang's Two Faces," *Far Eastern Economic Review*, 2 December 1999, 16–17.

⁷ Cited in William McGurn, *Perfidious Albion: The Abandonment of Hong Kong, 1997* (Washington, D.C.: Ethics and Public Policy Center, 1992), 37. McGurn's book remains the best single account of the Hong Kong handover.

⁸ "China's Town," *Asian Wall Street Journal*, 10 July 1990.

⁹ King C. Chen, *China's War Against Vietnam, 1979: A Military Analysis*, Occasional Papers/Reprints Series in Contemporary Asian Studies, no. 5 (Baltimore: University of Maryland School of Law, 1983). Nie Rongzhen, "Report to the Central Military Affairs Commission, February 1980," cited in *Inside China Mainland*, July 1980, 11. Chen Yun, "Speech to World Conference, April 1979," in *Inside China Mainland*, September 1979, 3.

¹⁰ Nie Rongzhen, "Report," 11. Chen Yun, "Speech," 3. Daniel Tretiak, "China's Vietnam War and Its Consequences," *China Quarterly* 80 (December 1979): 740–67, esp. 752–53.

¹¹ Henry Kissinger, *Years of Upheaval* (Boston: Little Brown, 1982), 50.

¹² Burr, ed., *The Kissinger Transcripts*, 309. Since China and the U.S. lacked common values and institutions, Kissinger was forced to rely on an essentially negative inducement—the Soviet threat—to draw China closer to the United States. Lucien W. Pye, "An Introductory Profile: Deng Xiaoping and China's Political Culture," *China Quarterly* 135 (September 1993): 412.

¹³ Burr, ed., *The Kissinger Transcripts*, 313–15.

¹⁴ Ibid., 384–85.

¹⁵ Ibid., 371.

¹⁶ For twenty years the official position of the U.S. government had been that Taiwan's future could only be determined through negotiations between Beijing and Taipei. In their very first meeting Kissinger told Zhou Enlai to ignore the official position, and spontaneously pledged that America would oppose an independent Taiwan. And he did so without extracting any concessions—such as the renunciation of the use of force—in return. See James Mann, *About Face: A History of America's Curious Relationship with China from Nixon to Clinton* (New York: Knopf, 1999)

¹⁷ See, for example, Goodman, *Deng Xiaoping*, 100.

¹⁸ For Deng himself, this marked a radical turnabout. In 1977, shortly after his return from political exile, Deng would still say that "In almost no likelihood will my generation or the generation of Comrade Hua Guofeng and Wang

Dongxing or even the following generation ever re-establish close contact with the Communist Party of the Soviet Union." Yet in subsequent years he laid the groundwork for the restoration of ties between the Chinese Communist Party and the CPSU. "Speech at 3rd Plenum of the 10th Central Committee," 20 July 1977, *Issues and Studies* (July 1978): 103.

[19] On December 10, 1998, Rep. Dana Rohrabacher (R-CA) traveled to Mischief Reef in the South China Sea on a fact-finding tour. He discovered evidence of a Chinese military build-up on the disputed islands, which form part of the Spratly Islands. The Associated Press reported on January 7, 1999, that China is altering its air force doctrine. According to the *China Reform Monitor*, no. 203 (17 May 1999), the DF 31, which was test-fired on August 2, 1999, will be deployed by 2002. See also *CRM*, no. 263 (10 December 1999).

[20] The story about Jiang and his generals is in Arthur Waldron, "Clinton's China Policy Invites Disaster," *Wall Street Journal*, 26 January 1999, A18.

[21] Yuan Hongbing, "Yi xin shijide mingyi," in Zhao Shilin, ed., *Fang "zuo" bei-wanglu* (Taiyuan: Shuhai chubanshe, 1992), 252.

[22] For this definition, see Liu Hong *et al.*, eds., *Zhongguo guoqing*, restricted circulation (Beijing: Zhonggong zhongyang dangxiao chubanshe, 1990), 3–8; cited in Geremie Barme, *In the Red: On Contemporary Chinese Culture* (New York: Columbia University Press, 1999), 446 n. 15. Emphasizing Chinese exceptionalism also helps to insulate the Middle Kingdom from subversive foreign ideas, like the notion of universal human rights. It enables the party to rebuff Western criticism of its human rights record by saying, in effect, that "here we have different standards." This was the tack taken by the official white paper on human rights published in 1991. See Guowuyuan Xinwen Bangongshi, *Zhongguode renquan Zhuangkuang* (The human rights situation in China) (Beijing: Zhongyang wenxian chubanshe, 1991).

[23] See "Aiguozhuyi jiaoyu shishi gangyao" (Policy outline for implementing patriotic education), *Renmin ribao*, 6 September 1994.

[24] Based on Churchill's paraphrase of *Mein Kampf*, as contained in his *The Second World War*, vol. 1 (New York: Houghton Mifflin, 1948).

[25] Leslie Chang, "In China, History Class Means an 'Education in National Shame,'" *Wall Street Journal*, 23 June 1999, A1.

[26] "Policy Outline," Section 1, Item 2. Barme, *In the Red*, 339–340.

[27] As Lucian Pye has observed, "Modern Chinese intellectuals have shown a passion for patriotism which has at each critical movement hobbled their political judgment," and "because they do not wish to seem unpatriotic, Chinese intellectuals have become more the lackeys of their political rulers than have the intellectuals in any other Asian countries." Lucian Pye, *Asian Power and Politics* (Cambridge: Harvard University Press, 1985), 193. This is not to suggest that China completely lacked intellectuals who were able to think independently and challenge authority, but rather that, because they were relatively few in number, they were easy to isolate and destroy when the government was intent on doing so. In Mao's China, intellectuals who breathed a hint of criticism paid a terrible price. Only the sycophants were left standing. He

Peiling, "Preface," *Zhongguo Keyi Shwo Bu* (China: just say no! *or* China can say no) (1996).

[28] "Evildoers Doomed to Meet Destruction" (in Chinese), *Renmin Ribao*, 15 May 1999. *Renmin Ribao*, 19 May 1999.

[29] *Beijing Qingnian Ribao* (Beijing youth daily), 19 May 1999. Lest one think that these sentiments owe their origin solely to the embassy bombing, a 1996 poll conducted by the China Youth Research Center showed that 90 percent of all Chinese youth—and 96 percent of college students—think the U.S. tries to dominate China. Eighty-four percent of Chinese youth believe that U.S. censure of China for human rights violations is "based on malice." See "China Can Say No to America," *New Perspectives Quarterly* 14., no. 4 (Winter 1996).

[30] The PLA had been solidly in favor of the Four Modernizations from the beginning, seeing it as a way to acquire advanced weaponry and bolster its firepower. Ye Jiangying and the other PLA marshals trusted that Deng, who was serving as Chief-of-Staff of the PLA in the seventies, would give the PLA pride of place in the modernization program. They supported him in the power struggles of the mid-to-late seventies, knowing that he shared their passionate interest in the creation of a modern, professional military capable of exerting itself beyond China's borders. The drubbing the PLA received at the hands of Vietnamese border units in the border war of 1979 showed how ineffective the "rifles plus millet" approach was on the modern battlefield.

[31] Su Kuoshan, "Road of Hope—Reviewing the Accomplishments of the '863' Project on the 10th Anniversary of its Implementation" (in Chinese), *Jiefangjun Bao*, 5 April 1996, reproduced in Foreign Broadcast Information Service, Daily Report, 8 May 1996, FBIS-CHI-96-089. The Cox Report contains an extended discussion of the 863 Program and its successor, the Super-863 Program. The 863 Program was billed as advancing the PRC's "economy and . . . national defense construction," but it was administered by the State Commission of Science, Technology and Industry for National Defense (COSTIND), and was designed to acquire advanced technologies in support of the PRC's military aims. See "PRC Acquisition of U.S. Technology," *U.S. National Security and Military /Commercial Concerns with the People's Republic of China* (Cox Report), vol. 1 (Washington, D.C.: U.S. Government Printing Office, 1999), 10–13. The Cox Committee, formally titled the Select Committee on U.S. National Security and Military/Commercial Concerns with the People's Republic of China, issued its classified report on January 3, 1999. A declassified report, from which many significant findings had been removed at the request of the Clinton administration, followed on May 25, 1999.

[32] Whether Jiang is trying to make up in military enthusiasm what he lacks in service credentials (unlike Deng, he never served in the PLA), or whether his appetites are simply expanding with China's ability to buy or steal modern weapons systems (the two tend to feed on one another), is difficult to say. Weapons acquired include 50 Sukhoi Su-27 jet fighters with the production rights for 200 more, two Kilo attack submarines, and four Sovremenny guided missile destroyers. Richard Fisher, "Foreign Arms Acquisition and PLA Modernization," Heritage Foundation Backgrounder, 1 June 1998. In late 1999 the PLA Navy announced plans to acquire two more Soviet destroyers.

[33] John Frankenstein and Bates Gill, "Current and Future Challenges Facing Chinese Defense Industries," *China Quarterly* 146 (June 1996): 394–427. "PRC Acquisition of U.S. Technology," Cox Report, vol. 1, 14. Wei Ke, "Army Re-Tools Commercial Production," *China Daily*, 17–23 August 1997.

[34] BBC Summary of World Broadcasts, Far East, 11 November 1992.

[35] As scrutiny of the PRC's military spending increases, additional pockets of spending are discovered, and estimates of the necessary multiplier grow. The World Military Expenditures Project of the Stockholm International Peace Research Institute (SIPRI) stated in 1992 that actual Chinese defense spending was anywhere from "two to four times higher" than official figures. A Department of Defense official was quoted the following year as saying that actual PLA expenditures were around $30 billion to $45 billion a year, at least five times the official budget. The Cox Report estimated that "actual military spending was four to seven times greater than official figures." Cox Report, Vol. 1, 17.

[36] Richard A. Bitzinger, "China's Defense Budget: Is the PLA Cooking the Books?" *International Defense Review*, February 1995, 36. See also Bitzinger, *"Off the Books": Analyzing and Understanding Chinese Defense Spending* (Washington, D.C.: Defense Budget Project, November 1994).

[37] For a detailed description of China's armaments programs, see Bill Gertz, *Betrayal* (Washington, D.C.: Regnery 1999), esp. chap. 5, "The Long March Forward."

[38] Office of Naval Intelligence (ONI) Report, quoted in Gertz, *Betrayal*, 104.

[39] John Pomfret, "China plans for a stronger air force; move reflects push to expand influence in Asia, serve notice to the United States," *Washington Post*, 8 November 1999, A17.

[40] William Triplett and Edward Timperlake have recently suggested that China might deploy nuclear-tipped missiles on the Sovremenny-class destroyers it is purchasing from Russia. The use of nuclear warheads on the eight supersonic SS-N-22 ("Sunburn") anti-ship missiles that each destroyer carries would significantly tip the balance of power in the Taiwan Strait by giving China the ability to wipe out an entire U.S. aircraft carrier battle group on first strike. See Triplett and Timperlake, *Red Dragon Rising* (Washington, D.C.: Regnery, 1999)

[41] Office of Naval Intelligence Report, quoted in Gertz, *Betrayal*, 104–5.

[42] Ibid., 105.

[43] Ibid.

[44] The reason this needs to be stressed is that, in recent years, the presumption seems to be working in the other direction. There seems at times to be a determined effort to overrule the "bean counters"—as if to minimize the China threat by minimizing the numbers of weapons themselves. When London's *Financial Times* reported on February 11, 1999, that China had produced 150 M-9 and M-11 missiles in 1998 and deployed most of them opposite Taiwan, the U.S. State Department immediately called the report into question. "Reports that suggest that there has been a sudden new deploy-

ment are wrong," said deputy State Department spokesman James Foley. "This is not a new threat; it stretches back for more than half a decade. . . . As part of its military modernization China has been deploying missiles for some time." *Washington Times,* 12 February 1999, A21. The original *Financial Times* story was based on "military analysts in Washington privy to a classified Pentagon report." The State Department countered with a lower estimate contained in a public report released in late 1998 by the National Air Intelligence Center, which estimated that fewer than 50 M-9s and M-11s had been deployed.

[45] See, for instance, Lin Changsheng, *Corruption in the PLA* (Claremont, California: The Claremont Institute, 1992).

[46] The PLA Military Commission declared in the mid-nineties that only army corps—not their constituent divisions, regiments, or battalions—may engage in entrepreneurial activity. Business privileges have always been reserved for logistics units; combat units are forbidden to go into business for themselves. These two directives helped to restrain PLA wheeling and dealing.

[47] Gertz, *Betrayal,* 106.

[48] Stephen J. Blank, *Challenging the New World Order: The Arms Transfer Policies of the Russian Republic* (Carlisle Barracks, PA: Strategic Studies Institute, Army War College, 1993).

[49] John Barry and Gregory Vistica, "The Penetration is Total," *Newsweek,* 29 March 1999. A Chinese agent working in Los Alamos National Laboratories allegedly stole crucial data on how to miniaturize nuclear weapons to enable up to ten weapons to be fitted into a single warhead. The theft took place in the mid-eighties, meaning that China has had a decade and a half to design, test and deploy these weapons on its existing ICBMs.

[50] James Risen and Jeff Gerth, *New York Times,* 6 March 1999, A1. See also George Melloan, "With Clinton in Check, China Flexes its Muscles," *Wall Street Journal,* 9 March 1999, A23.

[51] John J. Fialka, Congressional testimony, 17 June 1997. *Washington Post,* 15 February 1999, 16.

[52] The Russian connection makes these thefts all the more deadly, since China can design composite weapons systems, in which purchased Russian weapons platforms and stolen American technology both play a part. As the Cox Report warns, "The PRC's reported acquisition of solid-fuel and mobile missile launcher technologies [from Russia], if successfully combined with stolen U.S. nuclear design information, will enable the PRC to field a robust, road-mobile, inter-continental ballistic missile threat to the U.S. far sooner than would otherwise have been possible." "Overview," *Cox Report,* vol. 1, XXXV.

CHAPTER FIVE: The World Map of Hegemony

[1] Barry Buzan and Gerald Segal, "Asia: Skepticism about Optimism," *The National Interest,* 39 (Spring 1995): 83–84.

[2] See, for example, Barme, *In the Red,* 340.

[3] On the PRC's denunciation of President Lee see "Facts Speak Louder than Words and Lies Will Collapse on Themselves," *New China News Agency (NCNA)*, July 1999. In response to Beijing's saber rattling, Taiwan is moving to increase its defense spending. Republic of China Defense Minister Tang Fei recently testified before the Taiwan parliament on the need to counterbalance the growing PRC threat by upgrading the nation's anti-missile system, preparing against information warfare, and upgrading conventional combat power. "Tang Seeks Defense Budget Hike to Counter Mainland Threat," *Free China Journal*, 5 November 1999.

[4] People's Liberation Army sources recently claimed that, during the five-year period from 1995 to 1999, the strategic missile corps has achieved a 100 percent success rate. Cited in *China Reform Monitor*, no. 263 (10 December 1999), available at santoli@afpc.org

[5] Paul Bracken, *Fire in the East: The Rise of Asian Military Power and the Second Nuclear Age* (New York: Harper Collins, 1999), 58. According to the *Washington Times*, China was close to completing two short-range missile bases near Taiwan in late 1999. The bases, located at Yongan and Xianyou, will have about 100 new missiles capable of reaching all of Taiwan's major military bases with little or no warning. See Bill Gertz, "Clinton Concerned about Missile Threat," *Washington Times*, 9 December 1999.

[6] According to the Information Centre of Human Rights and Democratic Movement in China, the Chinese government detained at least 35,792 members of the Falun Gong between July 20 and October 30, 1999. "China Claims 35,000+ Arrests; Experts Say Number is Low," Reuters, 2 December 1999.

[7] Jasper Becker, *Hungry Ghosts: Mao's Secret Famine* (New York: The Free Press, 1996); see chap. 18, "How Many Died," for estimates ranging from 30 to 45 million.

[8] State Council, People's Republic of China, White Paper: *The One-China Principle and the Taiwan Issue* (Beijing: Taiwan Affairs Office, 21 February 2000). The white paper dismissed a requirement of the Taiwanese that political reform, that is, democracy and human rights, be added to the agenda for reunification talks. See Lee Teng-hui, *The Road to Democracy: Taiwan's Pursuit of Identity* (Tokyo: PHP Institute, 1999), for detailed exposition of the island's position.

[9] Although Beijing tried to defuse the dual nationality issue decades ago, it continues *de facto* in place. All Chinese, however many generations removed from the mainland, are considered to be "compatriots," possessing the right to take up residence in the land of their ancestors. By celebrating the Chinese race as the best and brightest in the world, the government is reinforcing a transnational identity that could form the future basis of irredentist claims on the territory of such states as Russia, Mongolia, and Kazakhstan.

[10] *Asiaweek*, 25 September 1994. *International Economy*, November/December 1996.

[11] *International Herald Tribune*, 25 August 1995, 5.

[12] James Billington, presentation at U.S. Institute of Peace Conference on Russia, Washington, D.C., 19 May 1999.

[13] See, for instance, Kuo-Kang Shao, *Zhou Enlai and the Foundations of Chinese Foreign Policy* (New York: St. Martin's Press, 1996), 160.

[14] "Tilting Towards America," "Intelligence" column, *Far Eastern Economic Review*, 22 July 1999.

[15] *The Nation* (Bangkok English-language daily), 31 March 1997; cited in Brzezinski, *The Grand Chessboard*, 168.

[16] Saydiman Suryohadiprojo, "How to Deal with China and Taiwan," *Asahi Shimbun* (Tokyo), 23 September 1996.

[17] Interview with Christopher Cox, 29 October 1999.

[18] When the presidents of China and Russia met with the presidents of several Central Asian republics in Kyrgyzstan in August 1999, for example, they pledged to create a "multi-polar world," a formula implying opposition to domination by the United States.

[19] "President Jiang Zemin has told a Japanese delegation that China will never intimidate other countries. . . . " Kyodo News Service, 6 May 1999.

CHAPER SIX: *Wuwei* is No Way

[1] Richard M. Nixon, *Beyond Peace* (New York: Random House, 1994), 127–128.

[2] See my *China Misperceived: American Illusions and Chinese Reality* (New York: Harper Collins, 1990) for a discussion of how American perceptions of China have fluctuated between the benign and the malignant for over a century.

[3] Matt Forney and Marcus W. Brauchli, "A Democracy Party Rises from the Ashes of Tiananmen Square," *Wall Street Journal*, 12 May 1998, A1.

[4] It is true that gains in income have been uneven, with the biggest increases coming in the cities, but it is safe to say that, with the exception of retirees living on a fixed income, almost everyone in China is better off today than they were two decades ago.

[5] Presidential veto message, 30 November 1989.

[6] "China in the Balance: The Case for Normal Trade Relations," Trade Briefing Paper no. 5, Cato Institute, 19 July 1999, 5. A more sober assessment was offered by Charlene Barshefsky, the U.S. Trade Representative, in speaking about the November 1999 WTO accord between the U.S. and the PRC that she negotiated in Beijing: "I am cautious in making claims that a market-opening agreement leads to anything other than opening the market. It may—it could have a spillover effect—but it may not. And we've got to understand that."

[7] For an account of the effort see Mann, *About Face*, 309.

[8] Susan V. Lawrence, "In Tiananmen's Shadow," *Far Eastern Economic Review*, 27 May 1999, 11.

[9] Barme, *In the Red*, 1.

[10] Some manuscripts denied publication without censorship are circulated privately as written, but their impact is limited. See Fong Tak-ho, "China: Academics Call for Democracy, Academic Freedom," *Hong Kong Standard*, 4 May 1998, 6.

[11] Kathy Chen, "As China's Restraints Ease a Bit, an Editor Copies Western Papers," *Wall Street Journal*, 21 July 1998, A6.

[12] "Beijing Cracks Down on Internet Challengers," *Washington Times*, 31 July 1998, A16. Internet companies have also been warned that they will be shut down if they publish "state secrets," a term so broad that it can be applied to almost any political statement whatsoever. Leslie Chang, "China Vows to Shut Web Firms Leaking 'State Secrets,'" *Wall Street Journal*, 27 January 2000, A14.

[13] Patrick E. Tyler, "Seeing China's Challenge through a Cold War Lens," *New York Times*, 14 February 1999.

[14] Quoted in *New York Times*, 21 April 1992, A10.

[15] *China Post* (Taipei), 26 August 1995, 2.

[16] *Can China's Armed Force Win the Next War?*, excerpts translated and published in Ross H. Munro, "Eavesdropping on the Chinese Military: Where It Expects War—Where It Doesn't," Orbis, 38 (Summer 1994): 355ff.

[17] Arthur Waldron, "Why China Could Be Dangerous," *The American Enterprise*, July/August 1998, 40.

[18] George Melloan, "China's Unspoken Goal is to Destroy American Power," *Wall Street Journal*, 11 May 1999.

[19] Quoted in Arthur Waldron, "Bowing to Beijing," *Commentary*, September 1998, 15.

[20] "China Arrests Bishop as Clinton Begins Visit," Catholic World News briefs, 26 June 1998.

[21] Erik Eckholm, "Three Who Urged Clinton to Meet with Democracy Groups are Detained; U.S. Protests," *New York Times*, 26 June 1998, A9.

[22] "China's Rude Reception," *New York Times*, 27 June 1998, editorial page.

[23] President Ronald Reagan told the dissidents at the U.S. embassy reception that "While we press for human rights through diplomatic channels you press with your very lives, day in, day out, year after year, risking your jobs, your homes, your all. . . . Coming here, being with you, looking into your faces, I have to believe the history of this troubled century will indeed be redeemed in the eyes of God and man."

[24] "Press Conference between President Bill Clinton and President Jiang Zemin," Federal News Service, 27 June 1998. The Chinese president, for his part, stoutly defended his government's longstanding positions, asserting that Tiananmen was not a mistake, Tibet is a part of China, and China enjoys the rule of law.

[25] By putting the U.S. squarely against "independence for Taiwan" and "membership in any organization for which statehood is a requirement," President Clinton capitulated on two further points. The official U.S. position, dating

from 1982, had simply been that the U.S. had no intention of pursuing a policy of "two Chinas" or "one China and one Taiwan." Anyone who reads English can see the difference between saying "We have no intention to perpetuate the existence of two states" and the Clinton compromise, which all but calls upon Taiwan to accept Beijing's terms for surrender. Neither does agreeing to help Beijing keep Taipei out of international organizations make economic sense. Why should Taiwan, with the 14th largest economy in the worth and monetary reserves second only to Japan, be excluded from the World Bank and the IMF if it chooses to join?

[26] "The Leaders' Remarks: Hopes for a Friendship, Even if Imperfect," *New York Times*, 28 June 1998. India was also rebuked. The Sino-U.S. Joint Statement on South Asia, issued by Jiang and Clinton following their summit meeting, represented a new and disturbing endorsement of China's ambitions to be the arbiter of Asian events. The first such joint statement to deal with a third country (excluding Taiwan), it criticizes the 1998 Indian and Pakistani nuclear tests. This particular issue is one on which Beijing, because of its past involvement in South Asian nuclear proliferation, has zero credibility. It was China's growing nuclear arsenal and diplomatic intransigence in the sixties and seventies that prompted India to develop nuclear weapons in the first place. In the years following, China went on to help Pakistan acquire its own nukes, building nuclear enrichment facilities, supplying ring magnets and other key technologies, providing blueprints for nuclear weapons, and transferring the missile technology necessary to deliver nukes. There was no little irony in asking China to join in condemning a nuclear stand-off that it had helped to create. In the event, Beijing was happy to reinject itself into the security situation in South Asia, this time not as a partisan and proliferator but—thanks to the U.S.—from a much loftier perch as the great power of Asia. New Delhi immediately attacked the statement as "hegemonistic"—which, as a description of China's ambitions in Asia, may not be far from the mark.

[27] Henry A. Kissinger, "A World of Changing Leaders, Struggling Governments and Strange Bedfellows, *Los Angeles Times*, 30 July 1989, Opinion section, 1. White House press conference, 24 January 1990. Robert S. Greenberger, "Bush Finds it Harder to Defend China Policy," *Wall Street Journal*, 17 May 1990, A20.

[28] Brzezinski, *The Grand Chessboard*, 151.

[29] Ibid., 54.

CHAPTER SEVEN: **Containing the Hegemon**

[1] "U.S. Admits Chinese Companies Helping Iran's Missile Program," Middle East Newsline, 10 May 1999 (worldtri@worldtribune.com, accessed 20 May 1999). John Maggs, "Secrets Shanghaied," *National Journal*, 29 May 1999, 1454. "Technologies Lost," *National Journal*, 29 May 1999, 1462.

[2] "Clinton Approves Sale of Missile Equipment to China," *New York Times*, 11 May 1999. "Clinton's New Computer Sale Risks Upgrading PRC Missile Strikes," Al Santoli, ed., *China Reform Monitor*, no. 263 (10 December 1999).

[3] "Stop Playing by China's Rules," Robert Kagan and William Kristol, *New York Times*, 22 June 1998, A23.

[4] Agence France Presse, Beijing, 9 August 1999.

[5] Michael Pillsbury, *Dangerous Chinese Misperceptions: Implications for DOD* (Washington, D.C.: Office of Net Assessment, Department of Defense, 1998), 24.

[6] "We ought to give them [China] whatever they want," Haig was advising the Pentagon by 1984. "They're not going to use it against us." Quoted in Mann, *About Face*, 133.

[7] Henry Kissinger, "Turmoil on Top," *Los Angeles Times*, 30 July 1989, 1.

[8] Michael Ledeen, "The Administration Quashes Truth Tellers on China," *Wall Street Journal*, 10 June 1999, A26.

[9] The quote is from Pillsbury, *Dangerous Chinese Misperceptions*, 14. "The evidence from an extremely large number of cases indicating that decision-making elites have been the victims of misperceptions is virtually overwhelming. What we know from these cases is that in a sizable number of instances, elite misperceptions appear to have played a crucial role in the decision to go to war. What we don't know, and perhaps can't know, is why these misperceptions occurred." Greg Cashman, *What Causes War? An Introduction to Theories of International Conflict* (New York: Lexington Books, 1993).

[10] Quotes are from Pillsbury, *Dangerous Chinese Misperceptions*, 14, 15.

[11] Asia lacks a sense of a common homeland, virtually ruling out a NATO-type organization any time soon. Rather, the U.S. has to be strong enough to be an attractive ally to each state individually. A military build-up in the East Asian region, even of modest dimensions, will help to offset the region-wide perception that the U.S. has no staying power. This will bolster existing alliances and help to create new ones with states bordering China that share our values and institutions. The U.S. should also be generous in sharing its intelligence resources and military technology with Asian allies, in order to shift the balance of power overwhelmingly towards democratic, free-market economies there.

[12] In early 1983, George Shultz, who had succeeded Alexander Haig as secretary of state, took a fresh look at the Kissinger-Haig policy of courting China as our chief strategic ally in the region. Shultz decided that prosperous, democratic Japan, not China, deserved that role. "We believe that democratic nations are more likely to follow the just and sensible polices that will best serve the future of the region and the globe," he declared in a San Francisco speech. As far as U.S.-China relations were concerned, "differences between our social systems" made close relations difficult.

[13] Burr, *The Kissinger Transcripts*, 186. State Council, People's Republic of China, White Paper: *The One-China Principle and the Taiwan Issue*, esp. p. 7.

[14] Warren Christopher's testimony before the Senate Foreign Relations Committee, 23 January 1993.

[15] The U.S. Department of State "China Country Report," released around the end of February each year, can be found at http://www.state.gov/www/ global/human_rights/1998_hrp_report/china.html.

[16] M. Bergere, "The Chinese Bourgeoisie, 1911–1937," in Fairbank (1983), 730.

[17] *Zhongshan Zongshu*, Vol. 4, *Xuanyan*, 2–3. Cited in Frank, 64.

[18] Fincher, 1981, 1.

[19] Chinese Ministry of Information, 1947: 589. PRC State Statistical Bureau, 1990: 706.

[20] We need make no apology for striving to maintain America's global primacy, the chief threat to which is the emergence of China as a hostile superpower. America's continued preponderance over China, as well as other states, brings with it important advantages for Americans. The benign American order carries benefits for the wider world as well by promoting prosperity, political development, and international peace. We should not be ashamed of asserting, with Samuel P. Huntington that "A world without U.S. primacy will be a world with more violence and disorder and less democracy and economic growth than a world where the United States continues to have more influence than any other country in shaping global affairs. The sustained international primacy of the United States is central to the welfare and security of Americans and to the future of freedom, democracy, open economies, and international order in the world." Can anyone doubt that Chinese primacy under the current PRC regime would threaten the security of the U.S., as well as the future of freedom, democracy, and international order in the world? Samuel P. Huntington, "Why International Primacy Matters," *International Security* (Spring 1993):83.

Index